with best wishes - Matthew

LES GRAHAM: *A Life in Racing*

Matthew Freudenberg

Published in 2006 by Charlton Publications
Orchard House, Creech St Michael, Taunton, Somerset TA3 5PF

Other publications by this author:

The Isle of Man TT – An Illustrated History
Aston Publications 1990

Negative Gravity – A Life of Beatrice Shilling
Charlton Publications 2003

ISBN: 0-9546165-2-9

Printed in England by Acanthus Press Ltd
Blackdown Business Park, Wellington, Somerset TA21 8ST
www.acanthuspress.ltd.uk

Contents

Les Graham – A Life in Racing

Acknowledgements

Foreword by Stuart Graham

Acknowledgements

My thanks for their patience, help and encouragement to the Graham Family: Stuart and Chris, Della, Jim, and to Barbara and Fred Bowers. Thanks also to motorcycle racers Rod Coleman, Cecil Sandford, Ken Kavanagh, Ken Dixon and Len Cramp.

For further technical and historical information, thanks to Harry Havelin, Bob Light, John Ogden and Annice Collett.

Many thanks also to Wendy, my wife, for her help, her many suggestions and her ruthless proofreading.

Most of the illustrations in this book are from the Graham family archive or the author's collection. Sources of all other images are acknowledged in the captions.

Finally, thanks to Joe Wood in Dublin and to Dave and Joan Crawford of Lisburn for their encouragement and help in providing links with journalists and riders with personal knowledge of Les Graham.

Foreword

By Stuart Graham

Over the years there have been numerous articles and features published about my father, and although the writing of a book has been suggested on several occasions, this is the first properly researched and detailed account of his life and career, including his wartime experiences as a Lancaster bomber pilot.

Matthew Freudenberg has painstakingly recorded my father's life, and with a great deal of family research, previously forgotten history and information has come to light. With the recollections of many of the people who knew him and raced against him, it is a fascinating and enlightening account of an historical era.

The story of a career interrupted by war is familiar to his generation, and explains why many early post-war heroes were of an age when modern sporting stars are considering retirement. I have always believed the qualities required to be a successful racer would prove useful in wartime, and having survived would make the risks in racing appear acceptable.

Whilst my brother Chris and I were still quite young when our father was killed, we do of course have happy memories of our family life with our parents. We accepted, as many youngsters do, our unusual and somewhat privileged lifestyle as reasonably normal.

Attending races, Continental travel and living in Italy in the 1950s was exciting , and having a famous father I am sure had many benefits. How our dear late mother coped with the aftermath of our father's death I can only imagine. We returned to England and she devoted herself to ensuring that we grew up in as normal a way as possible. We are indebted to so many people who were helpful and supportive during a traumatic period for our family.

For my mother, having to live with my own racing career must have been difficult, and I sometimes feel guilty, but she also felt a strange sense of pride, and knew that my father would have shared her feelings, as well as empathising with my wife.

We as a family are pleased that this fascinating and unique story has been published and we are all interested to learn things that, as in most families, no one thought to mention.

Despite having spent most of my life involved in motorsport, I am constantly surprised by the number of people who still talk about my father , and by the affection and high regard in which he is still held after all these years. He was taken from us early. We have missed growing up with him around and getting to know him better, but his reputation has always been our inspiration.

Les Graham at Wallasey beach for the sand races in 1930 or 1931. He is on the 500cc Rudge special with which he won many races in the Wirral and North Wales.

One

Wallasey Days

Robert Leslie Graham was born on September 11, 1911 in Wallasey, Merseyside. Wallasey, once a base for smugglers and wreckers, looks over the Mersey to the docks and civic buildings of Liverpool from the Wirral Peninsular. In 1911 fine sandy beaches stretched from Wallasey to the piers and funfairs of New Brighton, while inland the Wirral Plain meandered pleasantly to the seaside townlets of Hoylake and West Kirby. The villages in between were not yet swallowed up by development from Birkenhead, and the long straight road from Leasowe into Wallasey was ideal for informal speed-testing of powered vehicles.

The Graham family owned a combined dairy and grocer's shop in the busy "lanes" area of Wallasey. Other shops and residences crowded Rice Lane, but behind the Grahams' dairy were stables, sheds and grazing for the horses that pulled milk floats round Wallasey every morning. As Les and his elder brother, Versey, grew up, motorcycles and motorcycle bits took over some of the shed space from milk

floats. Versey, whose full name was George Andrew Versey Graham, also known as "Paddy", was only a few years older than Les, and when the latter passed his 14th birthday and acquired a motorcycle licence (5 shillings - no test) they "shared" the same motorcycle, an arrangement that was probably less straightforward than it sounds.

This motorcycle was an ancient Zenith Vee twin. As a self-taught engineer Versey kept it running, but with speed in their blood, both brothers would have tested its speed, and their nerves, on the long Leasowe straight. After Les, a sister, Irene was born to the Graham family, and finally a third boy, Richard. After Les followed Versey into organised motorcycle racing, their parents banned Richard from racing.

In 1928 Les bought a 350 Dot-Jap and entered it for racing at the Stanley speedway stadium in Liverpool. The little money he made fell far short of his expenses and when he was introduced to the circuit at Park Hall, near Oswestry, he found road racing more to

Park Hall circuit near Oswestry. Although short and narrow, Park Hall provided excellent racing for solo and sidecar racing. Les and his brother Versey were frequent competitors. *T.G. Bury, Birmingham*

his liking. This modest course, set in the grounds of a stately half-timbered hall that burned down in 1919, was only three fifths of a mile in length but managed to provide a combination of fast and slow bends and short sharp hills on a narrow tarred road. Races were organized by the Oswestry and District M.C. At Park Hall Les learned, very quickly, the skills and psychology of close racing. In spite of the narrowness of the track it was used for sidecar racing as well as solos; somehow the faster three-wheelers got past the competition.

In his first race at Park Hall in 1929, Les took second place on his Dot-Jap to local expert Harry Pinnington on an O.H.C. A.J.S. This remarkable result showed a talent well above the average, and was probably helped by some fast practice riding on quiet Wirral roads. The Dot was replaced by a 500cc Rudge assembled from a speedway Rudge engine and a standard 1926 Rudge roadster, and was good enough to win the trophy for fastest lap at Old Hall three years in succession. Not everything went Les' way though, and Len Cramp, a friend and fellow racer in the 30s, recalls an Easter meeting, when winter had still not made an exit. Les took the bend into Park Hall's short straight at something like his usual speed, and parted company with the Rudge on sheet ice. Bike and rider moved rapidly down the straight with Les

in the lead. Len noticed that Les was travelling on his back with arms and legs raised well clear of the track. Len asked an unhurt Les to explain this strange position and was told "I am not going to wear out my new leathers the first time I wear them!"

There were other events that Versey and Les took part in as often as their commitments to the dairy allowed. Wallasey sand races attracted large entries and large crowds, and there were one kilometre sprints as well on Harrison Drive, Wallasey's shoreside avenue. In 1932 C. P. Wood won both solo and sidecar sprints at 80.64mph and 76.09 mph respectively. There were very few road-racing tracks in Merseyside and the Midlands besides Donington, and no mountains for Continental-type hill climbs. Grass track racing, which started in earnest in 1927 on a disused golf course near Croydon, quickly won favour for close, hard-fought races on undulating field tracks, with good visibility for spectators and few rules. By 1930 there were nearly twenty tracks operating under club control, as well as occasional races held for charity or a festive event on a roped off area within a fete or public park. One such venue was the Roodee in Chester, an open area near the Dee where horse races and other public diversions took place. A race course was marked out of just over a mile's length and fierce competition and spiked tyres produced lap speeds of

A very young Les, wearing what look like jodphurs, before a race at Park Hall.

Versey Graham stands outside his cycle and motorcycle shop near the family dairy in Wallasey. Like Les he was a self-taught engineer. The shop became a popular meeting place for motorcycle racers and enthusiasts. The dog, Gip, was part of the establishment.

over 70 mph. Les was gaining a reputation as a man who was hard to beat, but as his Wallasey friend and competitor, Len Cramp, said, "He was wild when he wanted to be."

He was also very determined. Although he was a cheerful and good-natured competitor, he was absolutely single-minded as soon as he came under starter's orders. His line round any track was usually the fastest one, and he did not mind getting close to another rider to pass if the road was narrow. In 1933 Les was committed enough to racing to obtain a 348cc OHC Velocette on loan from Bill Dehaney, to back up the hard-used Rudge and enable him to compete in 350 class races. Although the Velocette was a 1925 model, it was expertly prepared, and swept the board in its class at Park Hall in 1933 and 1934. "Motorcycling" magazine had its reporter at Park Hall on Good Friday, 1934:

"The tit-bit of the meeting was the unlimited event in the first heat, when J. H. Inions (498 Special) clocked 4.29 for the five laps, equalling the fastest time up to that point of the afternoon. The second heat was comparatively slow, but the third was just the reverse. R. L. Graham (348 Velocette) had no walkover in his desire to keep ahead of E. R. Evans (499 Rudge) and for the first mile the latter refused to be "lost". Then

Graham broke away and roared round and round. Never losing a fraction of a second on the corners, he sent a thrill through neighbouring crowds when from time to time he took wide sweeps round the bends and skirted the grass. The announcement that he had beaten his own record with 4.26 came as no surprise to the onlookers. Graham was in winning mood and annexed the premier position in each of the three races in which he was entered."

Park Hall's organisers gave an unusual trophy to the winner of the day's fastest race; this was "the silk topper", a classic piece of headgear which showed the superiority of its winner.

Les finished school at fourteen. As soon as he could he had joined his brother in his bicycle and motorcycle repair shop, and by 1934 the business was well established. They had plenty of practice in repair and tuning from their racing activities, and the shop was popular. In 1935 Les met his future wife, Edna Hine, who was to support him at most of his races. She was often accompanied by her younger sister Barbara, who admired Les from the start and developed an interest in motorcycles and racing which she still has. At thirteen, Barbara thought that Les was "wonderful, very strong in character and full of enthusiasm about everything".

The "Silk Topper" awarded to the winner of the fastest race of each meeting at Park Hall being shown off by Les to the photographer, his future sister-in-law Barbara Hine.

An early shot of Les and Edna Hine, whom he married in 1937. Les had moved up to leather trousers at this stage, (1935 or 1936.)

Les was now one of the hardest man to beat on grass or tarmac in the North West. Where was he to go from here?

In 1936 a piece of luck helped Les to move up to major national road racing events. He heard that one of the overhead camshaft racing OK Supremes, with a damaged engine, was for sale at an affordable price. The price was more important than engine damage that had resulted from a dropped valve, and the bike was bought and rebuilt, and entered in the 250cc class of the Ulster Grand Prix to be held in August. Les still used his Rudge to win road and grass track events before setting off to Ulster for the "Prix", as it was known in Ulster.

The racecourse could not have been more different from Park Hall and other road courses in England. First used in 1922, it was a few miles from Belfast, held in open country and on public roads, as Ulster did not and still does not suffer from the ban on motor racing on public roads in place in England, Scotland and Wales. The course was twenty and a half miles long, triangular in plan, with a seven mile long stretch, the Clady straight. This notorious section could be taken flat out if the rider could withstand the bumps and the engine could stand the strain. It was an international event, but in 1936 the Italian, German and French entries for the Lightweight class all were non starters, leaving sixteen starters including Les.

In practice Les went well, posting third fastest time behind the New Imperial works riders, Les Archer and "Ginger" Wood on the first practice day. In the race, however, the engine failed, and the winner was Les Archer with Bob Foster (New Imperial) only feet behind after 205 miles of racing. Racing was resumed with the Rudge on grass tracks and sand while Les rebuilt the OK Supreme ready for a more ambitious programme in 1937.

The most important event for Les in 1937 had nothing to do with racing. He and Edna Hine were married in January, at St. Hilary's Church in Wallasey. His racing programme for 1937 was to be a test of stamina for Les and Edna with one, sometimes two events almost every weekend from Easter to the end of August. The faithful Rudge gave Les wins at early races on the grass and at Park Hall, but for the Cadwell Park road races on May 31 he started on a works entered 350cc OK Supreme. His efforts in Ulster had been noticed and John Humphries, a friend and grass track rival, who was also joint works manager at OK Supreme, provided a machine for the meeting. "MotorCycle's" reporter was there:

"The hero of the day was R. L. Graham, who practically swept the board on a works-entered OK Supreme... Riding his own beautiful race, Graham reduced the record time to 5 minutes 21 seconds for six laps. This was Graham's first appearance

Les on the 1925 OHC Velocette he rode on loan from Bill Dehaney from 1933 to 1936.

on Cadwell's concrete corners; when he went on to win the final from the redoubtable Lansdale (348 Velocette) he evoked a burst of cheers such as Cadwell has never heard before."

Les also raced for the first time at Donington in May, on what was the leading road-racing track in Britain. Little more than a woodland dirt-track when racing started in 1932, by 1937 it was a fine circuit over two and a half miles long. Versey and Les both entered the May meeting. Versey won the sidecar race, Les did not finish in either of his races. After a string of grass track races, the brothers were back at Donington on August Bank Holiday. This time Les was a winner, and Versey took fourth and fifth places in his races behind leading British sidecar pilots. Versey's outfit was made by Mr Grindley in Shropshire. He made several and called them Grindley - JAPs, causing some confusion with the earlier Grindlay Peerless-JAPs. There was no works 350 OK for Les this time, but he won his heat and fifth place in the 250 "Grand Prix" with his own OK Supreme, and took fourth place in the 20 lap 500 "Grand Prix" on the Rudge. Les seemed to have had a talent for making special parts and acquiring them from friends in the right place; his bikes had a sprightliness that matched his robust style.

A more down-to-earth aspect of the full programme of racing that both Graham brothers pursued was the

transport of their machines to events. In the twenties and thirties ingenuity and economy were the keynotes of moving racing machines to race tracks. The simplest method was to ride the racing machine itself to the place of competition: cheap, but this had strong risks of breaking down on the way or disagreeing with a policeman on the issue of noise. Some riders took their motorcycle by train to the station nearest the track; this could involve a long push between stations and for the final stretch to the course. This was Beatrice Shilling's chosen and exhausting method of getting from Manchester to Brooklands with her Norton. Most riders opted for the cheapest vehicle capable of carrying their machine. In 1935 Les Higgins shared an elderly Morris Cowley with a friend to carry his Velocette and the friend's Excelsior to Donington. "We had hoped to get the two bikes on to the luggage grid, a hope that was shattered, together with the luggage grid." Eventually the Excelsior rode inside the car after removal of front wheel and mudguard and the Velocette was lashed to the back, leaving Higgins and friend to squeeze painfully into what space remained - this arrangement got them to Donington! Les' young sister-in-law noted with interest that both Versey and Les followed a policy of rigorous economy in the choice of motorcycle hauler, generally using "light cars" rescued from collapse and repaired at the Kings Street shop. These were far from sturdy, and Barbara was pleased to note that Les' arrival at a track was usually marked by the door falling off his Swift.

The 1936 Ulster Grand Prix. Les, (83), on his own 250cc OK Supreme took advantage of the rain to catch up with the larger Nortons of Jimmy Hayes (43), and J. A. McClachlan (45), but he did not finish.

Works Rider

Les' most important race in 1937 was the Ulster Grand Prix. He was entered in the 250 class by Bill Stuart, owner of Stuart Motorcycle Depot in Blackpool, where Bill had the agency for most of the sporting makes, including OK Supreme. Stuart's experience as an engine tuner went back to 1920, and he worked with the OK factory in preparing their TT machines in 1936/37, as well as entering his own riders in major races. Les had the benefit of a fully-rebuilt and lightened machine for the 250 Ulster, rather than his own OK.

The race was dominated by Ernie Thomas, riding the only supercharged works DKW, but he matched his speed to the competition rather than blasting ahead to a massive lead. Tyrell Smith actually passed Ernie on the third lap, but Ernie repassed and led by 24 seconds at the end of the lap. The DKW was faster than many of the 350 machines that ran at the same time, but riders who tried to slipstream him generally let him get well ahead, so deafening was the bellow of the engine. (During pre-war TT races the DKW engine was said to be audible in Liverpool as it screamed down Bray Hill.)

Les Graham fought for third place with Les Archer, also a great rival in the mainland races at which they often met. Les led Archer's works New Imperial briefly, but finally took fourth place in a field of twenty leading riders. This was a good result for Les' second international class race, and Bill Stuart and OK Supreme were very pleased. Bill entered Les for another Ulster race, the "Belfast and District 100", to be held on September 18 on a new ten mile circuit at Comber in County Down.

September in Ulster suggests a probability of rain, and rain started after four laps and went on for the rest of the race. This was in fact an advantage to Les who had learned to adapt to rain, loose surfaces and outrageous bumps in his ten years experience of every type of racing from sand and grass to smooth road courses. He had ridden as fast as possible on all courses, sometimes faster than possible and falling off.

He won the 250cc class at Comber at a speed faster than all but two of the 350s and all but four of the 500s. OK and Bill Stuart were again very pleased.

Les at Donington, Easter Monday, 1939, where he finished third behind Harold Daniell and Johnnie Lockett, Nortons, riding a works 350cc OK Supreme, after leading for three laps of a closely-fought race.

John Humphries, friend, grass track rival and son of the chairman of OK Supreme asked him to join the company as works rider and development assistant, which meant tuning and assembling competition engines. He wanted an answer in time to enter Les in the 1938 250cc TT, and although we do not know OK's terms, they were good enough for Les to accept and prepare to move from Nantwich to be near the factory in Birmingham.

By 1938 the OK Supreme company was run mainly by members of the Humphries family. The founding father was Ernie Humphries, "Black Ernie", who with Charles Dawes set up in the cycle business in 1882, producing cycle components and complete "penny farthing" or "ordinary" bicycles. The "Black" characteristics of Ernie were an explosive rage and fearless rudeness. In 1926 he and Dawes parted company, and Ernie formed OK Supreme Motors Ltd, located in Bromley Street, Birmingham.

In 1928 an OK Supreme ridden by Frank Longman won the Lightweight 250cc TT, and another three OK Supremes finished in the first six places. This was a triumph for Ernie Humphries, who believed that racing was the best form of advertising, though sales figures did not confirm his belief.

The 1928 TT winner used a JAP engine fitted with a special cylinder head designed by George Jones and Ray Mason. Jones and Mason also designed the engines for OK's later overhead camshaft machines, the "Lighthouse" of 1930, and the more conventional OHC engine used from 1935 on the "Racing Camshaft" RC model as raced by Les Graham. This was offered to customers in 250cc and 350cc form, though the 350 was rarely raced by any but works riders.

Les joined OK in 1938 to help Pat MacIver, the young Technical Manager, develop and prepare engines for competition, and to ride for the company in road and grass track events. A big effort was to be made to win the Lightweight TT in 1938. John Humphries doubled as Competitions Director and joint Works Manager; the atmosphere at OK was usually stormy, not helped by John's fondness for provoking his father into one of his rages. Pat MacIver later recalled "I sat in at board meetings which often became hilarious." Ernie was very deaf and John provided a frivolous commentary on the Chairman's remarks. The business was largely held together by Ernie's daughters, Freida and Alie, Sales Director and Finance Director respectively, who had offered their services to bring some control to the volatile company.

Les started the 1938 grass track season at the Chester Club's Delamere Forest meeting on April 10. He won the 350, 600 and 1000cc races on a 350cc OK Supreme, presumably a works machine. At the Stratford Club's Bridgetown Farm event three weeks later, he won the 350 and 500cc classes. His

Les after the race at Donington with, right to left, his wife Edna, Alie Humphries and Major Bill Wilson, Senior Sales representative of OK Supreme. Alie was a director of OK and Head of Accounts. They all look very pleased.

own 250cc OK was not entered in any 1938 or 39 races; he called it "the creaking gate", and perhaps it was retired or sold on after its two busy seasons. Les missed the opening grass meeting of the Salop Club at Monkmoor Aerodrome, Shrewsbury, on May 8, 1938. John Humphries, Andy Mackay and Freddie Hudson rode works 350 OK Supremes, but were beaten by C. Mead on his Mead Special. In the sidecar class, Versey Graham won the final after a race-long tussle with A. R. Bateman, Velocette.

Practicing for the TT races started at the beginning of June. Six OK Supremes were entered in the 250cc race, four of them by the OK company and two by Bill Stuart, who had entered Les in the Ulster Grand Prix in 1937. There were worries about the fragility of the valve mechanism of the OHC machine, and Ernie Humphries and Pat MacIver applied themselves to strengthening it. Ernie acquired a cylinder head design intended to reduce sidethrust on the valves. Pat had to design and machine all the special parts to allow them to be fitted on the four racers entered for the TT. Les was not involved in this development as he was needed to build customer racing engines, so MacIver was on his own and working until dawn to beat the TT deadline. It was only when the new engines had

been fitted and road tested that Ernie admitted that the new valve spring arrangement was covered by patents which he had not paid for, and under threat of legal action, he told an appalled MacIver that he would have to start again. Pat MacIver related in a postwar magazine article that he was so tired and depressed that he only reported for work a day and a half later, after considering quitting the company on the spot.

To his surprise and relief he found Les well under way with preparing the first two TT machines with old type engines that he had reworked, and Les himself took them over to the Isle of Man in time for the first practice. The other two were shipped across two days later. Pat prepared to fly to the Island with John Humphries but Ernie refused permission. Pat had had enough: he gave in his notice.

As well as Les, the OK Supreme team for the TT comprised Walter Rusk, the fearless Belfast rider, returning to racing after two years of waiting for a badly broken arm to heal; Putt Mossman, an American described as a stunt rider, and G. Stone, riding on the Isle of Man for the first time. Total entries for the 1938 Lightweight were thirty, including teams from

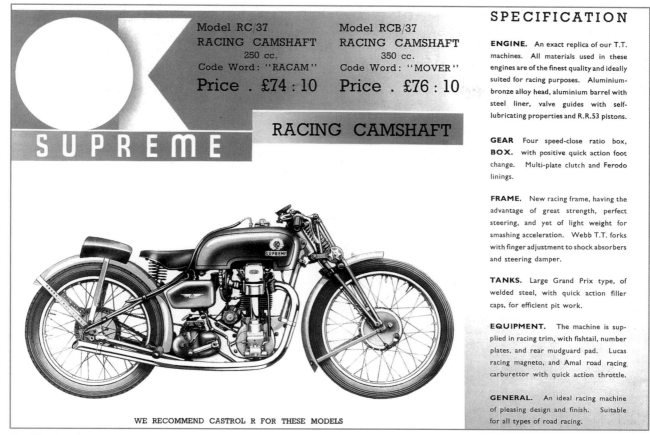

SPECIFICATION

ENGINE. An exact replica of our T.T. machines. All materials used in these engines are of the finest quality and ideally suited for racing purposes. Aluminium-bronze alloy head, aluminium barrel with steel liner, valve guides with self-lubricating properties and R.R.53 pistons.

GEAR BOX. Four speed-close ratio box, with positive quick action foot change. Multi-plate clutch and Ferodo linings.

FRAME. New racing frame, having the advantage of great strength, perfect steering, and yet of light weight for smashing acceleration. Webb T.T. forks with finger adjustment to shock absorbers and steering damper.

TANKS. Large Grand Prix type, of welded steel, with quick action filler caps, for efficient pit work.

EQUIPMENT. The machine is supplied in racing trim, with fishtail, number plates, and rear mudguard pad. Lucas racing magneto, and Amal road racing carburettor with quick action throttle.

GENERAL. An ideal racing machine of pleasing design and finish. Suitable for all types of road racing.

Model RC/37 RACING CAMSHAFT 250 cc. Code Word: "RACAM" Price . £74 : 10

Model RCB/37 RACING CAMSHAFT 350 cc. Code Word: "MOVER" Price . £76 : 10

OK SUPREME

RACING CAMSHAFT

WE RECOMMEND CASTROL R FOR THESE MODELS

The "Racing Camshaft" model OK Supreme, as shown in the sales catalogue for 1938. The model did not live up to its purposeful appearance and was dropped for 1939.

the New Imperial, Excelsior, Rudge, DKW and OK Supreme companies, as well as individual Cotton, Terrot and CTS entries. The race was not a happy one for OK. Les finished twelfth and gained a Bronze Replica, Stuart's entry, S.M. Miller, finished tenth, and none of the remaining OK riders finished. The OHC engine once more showed its lack of stamina.

On July 10 Les was at the Rushmere hill climb and grass track, facing the best riders in the Midlands. Rushmere was a roller-coaster of a track, near Bridgenorth, with steep rises and descents providing spectacular racing. The meeting began with a knock-out competition up Rushmere Hill in pairs, ending with the two fastest in each class meeting in a final race. Les reached the 350cc final racing against the fast and experienced Dick Tolley on a KTT Velocette. Fortunately for Les, Tolley forgot to turn on his petrol. "By the time the juice was flowing again it was too late and Les was over the top to win in 15.4 seconds." Tolley kept the juice flowing in the 350cc grass track final and won from Les, who rode fiercely on his first visit to the track.

In the last heat for the unlimited solo final, Les was caught out on the unfamiliar course and crashed

at speed, breaking his collar bone. The accident finished his racing in what was a disappointing year. OK Supreme withdrew the overhead camshaft racers from their range for 1939 and offered a JAP engined machine, the RRS/39, adapted from the purpose-built GTS/39 grass track racer, for racing on road tracks or at Brooklands. The TT and other international races were not in John Humphries' competition programme for 1939.

Part of Les Graham's job at OK Supreme was the assembly of racing engines and their preparation for whatever kind of racing was their end use. Grass track and most Brooklands engines ran on methyl alcohol fuel; road racing engines ran on a 50/50 petrol - benzol mixture. OK publicity claimed that the racing engines were specially made for them by JAP; strengthened crankcases with cooling fins suggests that this was so, though poetic licence was known to creep into the company's publicity.

Ernie Humphries seems to have kept advertising spending to a minimum, judging by the little that appeared in the motorcycling press. However he was generous with press releases and opportunities for journalists to try new models. Early in March 1939,

Johnnie Lockett on a 348cc Norton at Donington in 1939. He and Daniell were lent machines by Norton while the company dropped racing in that year. *T.G.Bury, Birmingham*

"Motor Cycling" magazine was offered an extensive trial of the GTS racing machine, in grass track tune at Lilleshall, and at Donington in road racing form. Alec Menhinick was the reporter, and at Lilleshall John Humphries was host and demonstrator. Humphries' warm - up on the track gave Menhinick second thoughts about a ride: "The model seemed only occasionally to be in touch with the ground and looked more like a giant grasshopper at speed than anything else."

Menhinick tried the machine none the less and was impressed by the stability and acceleration of the GTS, finding second gear quite quick enough for the dry, shingly surface of the track. Converted overnight to run on petrol/benzol, and demonstrated by Les and John Humphries, the machine's behaviour at Donington encouraged the reporter to use more of its pace, and in both forms he gave it his enthusiastic approval.

Les was without a suitable machine when the entry list for the 1939 TT opened. To keep within sight of the supercharged Moto Guzzi and DKW 250s, the road racing version of the OK GTS would have to be tuned beyond the limits of reliability and was not an option. Les heard that Ron Harris, the fastest of the Brooklands semi-road track riders, who never entered the TT, had a fast Velocette available, but he was beaten to the draw by Walter Rusk. Chris Tattersall, who had been riding his own Rudge engined CTS

machines in TTs since 1931 fortunately had one to spare for Les.

There were several grass track and road events in which Les was to ride a works 350 OK Supreme before the TT. The first of these was the Easter Monday meeting at Donington. Harold Daniell and Johnnie Lockett were entered on ex-works 1938 Nortons, Norton having withdrawn from racing for economic reasons, and were expected to dominate the opposition. It cannot have been a total surprise that Les made one of his lightning starts and shot into a lead of several hundred yards before the Hairpin Bend. It was more surprising in view of the Nortons' much higher speed on the straights that Les held them off until the third lap, and broke the existing record eight lap time, finishing third behind Lockett and Daniell. Titch Allen, elder statesman of the Vintage Motor Cycle Club, was a spectator at Donington and remembers Les "taking Redgate Corner in a speedway slide."

Jock West had entered a BMW in the 500 race at Donington but did not start. He watched Les and was highly impressed by his forceful and fearless style, though by now Les was recognised as a most competitive rider. Jock determined to sponsor Les on a Velocette in the major road races of 1940. It was not to be, but Jock did not forget what he had seen. Meanwhile Les fitted a meeting at Cadwell in between his preparations for the TT. He won the 350,

The fearless Irish rider Walter Rusk was one of OK Supreme's entries in the 1938 Lightweight TT. This was his first TT since 1935, when he was 2nd in the Junior and 3rd in the Senior on works Nortons. *FoTTofinder Archives*

500 and unlimited races on his 350cc OK Supreme in spite of a coming together with George Brown, Vincent HRD, and getting up and restarting to win in the last event.

Les cannot have been very hopeful when he set sail for the Isle of Man with the CTS. He had seen (and heard) the works DKWs at Ulster and knew that they and the Italian works machines had at least ten miles per hour advantage over him. The TT is too fast a course to enable the best rider to make up the difference, specially when riders like Stanley Woods, Ernie Thomas and Ewald Kluge were riding the continental entries.

As it happened, heavy rain during the 1939 Lightweight TT gave Les an opportunity to exceed the CTS' potential, and he worked his way up to fourth place on the fifth lap before his engine failed. Mellors won on the Benelli, followed by Kluge, DKW, and Tyrell – Smith, Excelsior – another man who was quite happy on wet or loose surfaces.

Almost every weekend from his return from the TT right up to the end of July, Les was racing and winning for OK Supreme at grass tracks across the North -West and Midlands. He did not quite have it his own way every time and was occasionally beaten by fellow OK riders Andy MacKay and Freddy Hudson, or by Bob Foster (New Imperial), Stan Hindley (Velocette KTT), and the very successful

Dick Tolley on a KTT that was said to be a gift from a loving grandmother. By late summer most "grass tracks" were rock-hard mountain dirt tracks, very fast, very bumpy. Straights were long enough for riders to "tuck in" flat on the tank, and monowheeling out of corners was the norm.

In spite of occasional defeats, Les was probably the fastest rider on the grass tracks in 1939; his last event before the war was at Layhams Farm, down country in East Wickham, Kent. Here the organisers of the Southern Counties Championship had invited Midlanders to fight out the championship with them, so Les, MacKay and John Humphries were to meet the hard men of the South, including Eric Oliver, Les Schweiso and Wally Lock. Les won the newcomers' race from his OK teammates. Wally Lock pushed inside Les to win the 350 Final, but in the Southern Counties Championship 16 lap race Les was on best form. "With a terrific sweep round Fowlhouse corner and a crashing sprint down the straight, Graham was leading the battle again." – reported "Motor Racing". Les won the final, the Championship and the "100 Guineas Matchless Trophy."

Events organised for August and September were being advertised by their organisers, and the hopeful competitors were already in the Isle of Man for the Manx Grand Prix, when the government announced a state of war with Germany on September 3rd. There was to be no more racing for seven years.

In the absence of a suitable OK Supreme, Les borrowed one of Chris Tattersall's Rudge-engined CTS machines for the 1939 Lightweight TT. It did not last the course. *FoTTofinder Archives*

A close group at the fast Lilleshall grass track. Les Graham, (18, works OK Supreme) chases Jack Lowe on a "customer" OK Supreme GTS/39. Les was on top form throughout 1939, winning somewhere almost every weekend of the Summer and taking the Southern Counties Mountain Grass Track Championship at Layham's Farm in Kent. *T.G.Bury, Birmingham*

One of the most exciting OK Supreme riders was Andy Mackay, a Merseysider from Birkenhead. He is in action at the Evesham Club's Fish Hill track in June, 1938. *T.G.Bury, Birmingham*

Dick Tolley on a very fast OHC Velocette was probably the hardest man to beat for Les and the OK team. With calm concentration he has started down the notorious hill at Rushmere in a high-speed slide to hold off second place man, "Happy" Smith, Ariel. *T.G.Bury, Birmingham*

John Humphries shared his father Ernie's belief in the value of racing for publicity and development. He invited Les to join OK Supreme and was a very successful rider himself. Here he is at Maxstoke Castle in September 1939, the sunburst badge of OK Supreme visible on his tank. *T.G.Bury, Birmingham*

Freddie Hudson was another very fast OK team rider. As well as winning countless grass track events, he was a successful rider on the Isle of Man. He was 3rd in the 1936 250cc Manx Grand Prix, entered by Bill Stuart, and after the war he was sixth in the 1947 Junior TT on a Norton. Here at Lilleshall he shows off the new Grass Track Special, (GTS/39) introduced by OK Supreme in 1939. With a well-tuned JAP engine, it was very hard to beat. *T.G.Bury, Birmingham*

Flying Officer Graham, rear right, and his crew relax in front of their Lancaster at Kirmington, base of 611 Bomber Squadron. As usual, most of them are smoking as they sit on a pile of bombs.

War Service in the Royal Air Force

When war broke out Les Graham was across the channel, on a mission to Eastern Europe described as an "Army sales promotion". Whatever this was, it found him in Hungary at a very awkward time, but somehow he managed to return to England and carry on working for OK Supreme.

On March 3rd 1942 Les reported for duty in the Royal Air Force at his Air Crew Reception Centre. This was the first of twelve training establishments he was to pass through before he was posted to his combat squadron, two years and two months later. It would be four months before he started any flying training, and then, if he passed all his exams, he would move on to specialised courses for the type of aircraft he would fly in active service.

1941 had been a year of German successes; the German occupation of most of Europe was followed by a rapid invasion of Russia and the domination of North Africa with most of the Mediterranean. The strength and courage of Fighter Command and the strength of the Navy made Hitler abandon his plans to invade Britain, but Britain and her few fighting allies were now on the defensive on all fronts. A realistic plan of attack on Germany was essential to slow the enemy down.

The Chiefs of Staff of the Army, Navy and Air Force debated, then decided: the attack on Germany would be by air, by Bomber Command, and under new leadership in the person of Air Chief Marshal Sir Arthur Harris. Harris, appointed in February 1942, believed that better aircraft, chiefly the Lancaster, and a new strategy of large bomber forces concentrating on one target, would destroy civilian morale and weapons production in Germany. This objective was defined by the Chiefs of Staff, and did not originate with Harris, as is sometimes thought; he approved it and put it into effect.

At thirty-one, Les was too old to be considered as a fighter pilot. Nevertheless a standard elementary flying training lasting four months was given to all

Side view of a Lancaster above the clouds. The Lancaster was a favourite of test and operational pilots for its responsive handling and adequate power, courtesy of four Rolls Royce Merlin engines.. A Lancaster was once deliberately rolled through 360 degrees by test pilot Alex Henshaw, a frightening thought. In spite of its size the Lancaster was not an easy aircraft to move around in, and the tail gunner was quite isolated once he had crawled through his tunnel to the rear. *Royal Air Force Museum*

potential pilots. The de Havilland Tiger Moth, with its top speed of 100mph, was the safe and long-suffering aircraft in which most trainees first flew, and did their "circuits and bumps." The successful trainees were then posted to an Air Crew Dispersal Centre where they were told in which Command of the Royal Air Force they would serve. Les was posted on to train in Canada, at Monkton, New Brunswick. This was another Elementary Flying Training School, but less elementary than the first, and here Les learned of the joys and pitfalls of multi-engined aircraft.

Of the 55,000 thousand bomber aircrew who died during the war, over 8,000 died from accidents, and most of these died while training. Two of the perils common to twin-engined aircraft were: firstly, because both engines rotated their propeller in the same direction, the aircraft had a tendency to swing off line once take-off commenced, and the more powerful the engine the worse the swing. Crosswinds compounded the need for delicate while firm correction. Secondly, multi-engined aircraft usually had a complicated arrangement of fuel tanks and taps; switching tanks in the wrong sequence could leave the engine without fuel, which a low-flying pilot could discover too late.

Les spent nine months in Canada, flying Airspeed Oxfords and practising navigation, instrument flying, bomb-aiming and radio operation, as bomber pilots

were expected to be able to take over any other crew task if necessary. He liked Canada and Canadians, and was a leader of his fellow trainees in social high spirits. Organised sport was not his favourite activity, and he volunteered for netball as he believed that this "women's game" would be harmless. A broken collar-bone suffered while playing changed his mind.

He came back to England to "convert" to heavy bombers - Wellington and Halifax - and to form his own crew for service with a combat squadron. This Les did during a course at 18 Operational Training Unit at Finningley in Yorkshire, attended by future aircrewmen who had completed training as gunners, radio operators, flight engineers, bomb aimers or navigators. A day was set for pilots to gather the men who would fly with them on the basis of a few days' knowledge of the other course members.

Les formed a close friendship with his navigator, Bill Bissonnette, a Canadian who was ten years younger, and who has passed on clear memories of service with Les from Canada where he lives today. "At that time I was 22 and Les was 33. We started flying as a crew on Wellingtons on Dec. 9, '43 and flew almost 100 hours before going to Sandtoft where we flew about 30 hours on Halifaxes while Les got used to the extra two motors. We went to Lancaster Finishing School at Helmswell and added another 10 hours on Lancasters. On May 25 we were posted to

Les receives his pilot's wings at the end of the first stages of flight training in Canada. He still had training on multi-engine and heavy aircraft to come.

Kirmington (166 Squadron) and did a couple of night cross country trips so the Wingco knew we could fly a Lanc."

Satisfied with their fitness for combat, Wing Commander Donald Garner gave Les' crew one week's leave. They had been told that they would have a tour of duty of thirty sorties or operations, then after a break on non-combat duties, a second tour of twenty operations. In fact the second tour was never made compulsory because of the high level of casualties among bomber crews, but early in 1945 the number of "ops" on the single tour was increased to 36, as bombing had reduced the power of German cities to retaliate.

Their first operation was as part of a massive bomber stream of over a thousand aircraft on "D" day, to attack road and railway communications inland of the Normandy landings, to obstruct German troop movements in the area. Number two, the next night, was a raid on similar targets, but this time there was a fierce counter - attack by German night fighters. Two Lancasters from 166 Squadron were shot down and Les' aircraft was among those more or less lightly damaged by flak. A total of 28 bombers were lost from the 337 that set out..

The variety of targets attacked by 166 Squadron during Les' service was greater than that of many

other units. They included road and rail links, German tank and artillery positions, V1 "doodlebug" launch sites, Luftwaffe fighter bases, the synthetic fuel manufacturing plants so crucial to German land and air movement, and E and U boat pens in northern France. Many of these targets were still well defended, and during Les' tour of duty, twenty-six aircraft failed to return from operations to 166 base at Kirmington, representing a loss of 182 men, or over 50% of the Squadron's aircrew strength.

To list each of Les' sorties would be an excessive and probably tedious deviation from the story of a motorcycle racer, but a few of the most eventful showed personal qualities which civilian life does not usually reveal. On June 12 and June 16 the squadron attacked synthetic oil plants in the Ruhr industrial region, on each occasion with 300 other bombers. The first raid on Gelsenkirchen was most accurate and crippled the plant for several weeks. However so much smoke was created by the burning oil that some confusion followed and three of 166 Squadron's Lancasters were shot down by night fighters. The second raid took off in spite of cloud over the target, resulting in inaccurate bombing and heavy losses to night fighters and anti-aircraft gunfire or "Flak." Squadron Leader Garner reported that eleven bombers were seen to be shot down in flames.

Two sorties of special importance were described by

The "Oswald" pub in Scunthorpe served as the local for Les and his crew. It had a band and audience participation. In this photo Les is performing with maraccas and probably inciting the crowd to join in.

Bill Bissonnette. The first was an attack on railway marshalling yards at Revigny in France, when 166 Squadron sent 29 aircraft to join another 350, covering several railway targets. Bill relates:

"Revigny was our 16th op., where we nearly got it and where I put the kibosh on the saying that when you think you are about to die your whole life passes before your eyes. The night was July 12 and when we arrived at the target area after a flight of over four hours, the Pathfinder force had it well lit up with parachute flares, but were unable to put down the Target Indicator flares, to which the master bomber would direct us. On this trip he advised us that they had dropped a green T.I. a mile or so from the target area and we were to orbit this until they could identify the target and issue instructions.

"On a Lancaster the pilot was the only crew member with a seat belt and it consisted of two sturdy straps over his shoulders. After four hours of flying Les' shoulders were quite sore so he had unfastened the straps. I was not in my seat but standing behind Les, and Roy Lakin the bombardier was lying on his stomach behind the bomb sight waiting for the master bomber's instructions when all of a sudden we were upside down and hurtling toward the ground. As we flipped over, Les, without his seat belts done up, spilled into the centre of the aircraft and I thought our end had come.

"Les was scrambling about, draped over the throttles and trying to reach the stick, finally got his left hand on it and managed somehow to pull us out of it. Just about this time the master bomber called up the bomber force with instructions to abandon the mission and Les said to me; "Bill give me a course quick and let's get out of here." Naturally when the plane tumbled like that our gyro compass had also tumbled and wouldn't work so I looked out of the astrodome and spotted the Big Dipper which everyone knows points to the North Star, so I instructed Les - "See the Big Dipper - keep it on your right until I get the compass reset."

"Now getting back to the part about thinking you are about to die. As officers we had to buy our own clothing. I needed a new pair of dress shoes but naturally in wartime England there were none available. Roy Lakin, our bomb aimer, said: "I'll get you a pair, I know a girl in clothing stores," and sure enough that morning he presented me with a fine pair of dress Oxfords. As we hurtled toward the ground to certain death, I was sure, the thought running through my mind was "Guess I'm never going to wear those shoes.""

"When we got back to Kirmington there was dense fog and we were diverted to Wittering where we got down safely, 9 hours, 20 minutes after setting out. As

The navigator in Les' aircrew, Bill Bissonnette, became a close friend of Les, keeping contact after the war and visiting the Grahams in England. He lives in Thunder Bay in Canada and provided the first-hand accounts of bomber operations in this book.

we sat around the mess at Wittering we told our story of the upside-down Lancaster and how we couldn't figure out how it happened and a gunner from another crew said "I saw it happen – a night fighter blew up a Lanc that was directly beneath you and when his bomb load blew up - over you went." Maybe Les got the Distinguished Flying Cross for that one or maybe the perfect landing he made at Carnaby with a flat tyre on the starboard wheel."

On this later sortie to a night fighter base in France, German flak was heavy and damage to one of the wheels was spotted on the return journey. Les ordered his crew to take up crash positions - braced against something solid and facing the rear. Bill recalls "Somehow Les managed to drop the port wing so it barely cleared the ground and landed the Lanc like a bicycle on the port wheel and the tail wheel." It was a skillful piece of flying, and Les' ability had already been recognised by promotion to Flight Lieutenant from August 1, 1944. Toward the end of his tour of duty, Les was lead pilot when the Squadron took off . His last sortie with the Squadron was to Stettin, main German port for the Russian front, a round trip of 8 hours, 40 minutes, on which one of 21 aircraft from 166 Squadron was lost.

Les completed thirty flights in less than three months. Many sorties were on consecutive nights or days, almost all met flak and enemy fighters and in many there were losses from his own squadron. His crew must have felt relief and some gratitude to Les that they had all survived. Like many front line servicemen he almost never spoke about his experiences at home, and he dismissed his DFC as "just one they had left over at the end." In fact it was awarded in December, 1944, "for courage and devotion to duty whilst flying in active operations against the enemy," and posted in the "London Gazette" on the 8th of that month.

From 166 Squadron Les moved on to long distance flying with Transport Command. First he practiced blind landings using Radio Range Beams, an approach between converging radio beams which each gave out different audible signals, though by late 1944 radar was in use elsewhere for blind landing as well as enemy aircraft detection. Les was then posted to 232 Transport Squadron at Stony Cross to fly Stirlings to the Far East. The Short Stirling had four fourteen-cylinder sleeve valve Bristol Hercules radial engines. It existed in bomber and transport versions and its cruising speed was 230 mph.

Les flew an aerial bus route to Karachi via Castel Benito, Cairo, Lydda and Shaibah, taking a day for each stage. His first flight, after local day and night flying to get to know the aircraft, took off on March 12 1945, and finished at Karachi on March 16. The return usually took longer, and for variety he occasionally flew to Poona or Dum Dum airfield at Calcutta. There was some compensation for this routine in the chance to see something of India and its people and to bring home carpets and other gifts. Otherwise the routine went on with a break for another course of blind landing training, and the introduction of Avro York transport aircraft to replace the Stirlings. The York was fitted with four Rolls Royce Merlin engines.

The war in Europe ended with German surrender on May 7, 1945, and "VJ" day, the surrender of Japan came on August 14 in that year. Once the celebrations were over the chiefs of each of the services had to reduce their fighting units after most servicemen were demobilised, keeping in mind what risks of war they thought remained. Around this time Les was transferred to 511 Transport Squadron to continue with his long hauls to India. Servicemen serving in the Far East were the last to go home, some a full year later than the majority. Les was finally "demobbed" on July 29, 1946. Les had snatched every opportunity to get home to Edna on leave and now he had two little boys, Stuart and Christopher, born in 1942 and 1945. It must have been a very special day.

The Graham brothers with their wives and children, probably in 1947. The couples from left to right are: Les and Edna, Richard and Della, and Versey and Mabel, and the children, left to right are Stuart and Christopher, Ian and Veda, and Andrew and Jim.

1946 The Return of Racing

Racing restarted surprisingly soon after the war, considering the severe shortage of fuel, lack of spares and new tyres and the damage done to many race tracks by army and air force installations. Riders were eager to go, many tracks reopened, and racing motorcycles reappeared from dusty sheds or, in the case of France and Italy, from the barns and cellars where they had been hidden from occupying troops. Easter 1946 saw race events in England, France, Switzerland and Italy. Switzerland and Italy even ran international Grands Prix.

Les managed to arrange leave from 511 Squadron, which he shared between his family and the postwar reopening of Cadwell at Easter. From somewhere he obtained a Norton and won the 350cc final on it from one of his old grass track rivals, Eric Oliver. Jock West had wanted to enter Les in the 1940 TT on a Velocette, but after a busy war as commanding officer of a large aircraft repair and upgrading unit, Jock accepted a job at Associated Motorcycles – AJS and Matchless – as Sales Manager with

responsibility for the competition department. He now wanted Les as an AJS works rider and tried to locate him while Les was still in the RAF. Jock West was demobilised before Les and found him, the story goes, by putting a letter in "Motor Cycle" magazine, which an RAF friend spotted and passed on to Les. AJS had a brand new 500cc racing twin cylinder machine under development and with it they hoped to knock spots off Norton and Velocette, who were refurbishing their prewar designs.

Les accepted the offer from AJS but before starting work entered the first post war race on the Clady circuit in Ulster on August 17th. The course was reduced from its original 21 miles to 16.5 by the building of two airfields at different points on the circuit during the war. The bone-shaking seven mile Clady straight remained, though many riders would not have grieved if another airfield had shortened it. The Ulster Road Race was not a Grand Prix, and doubts about the quality of the wartime synthetic rubber tyres used by most riders were spectacularly

A road race in Italy in 1946. The enthusiasm of crowds returning to watch motor racing for the first time since the war the war was unchecked by most race organisers and spectators thought nothing of stepping into the road to see what was coming.

justified by events. A good start which saw Artie Bell lead Les, Bill Beevers, Rex McCandless and the rest was followed by a rapid first lap, then a shower of disintegrating synthetic rubber as Artie raced by to start his third lap. Les' engine gave up and further tyre and engine failures reduced the field of 13 to the one final finisher, B. M. Graham.

Meanwhile, the F.I.M., the international federation governing motorcycle racing, threw a large spanner into the work under way at AJS to develop a new 500cc racing engine. This engine was planned as a supercharged triple back in 1939 by Harry Collier, son of the founder of the Matchless company, and its progress, if it can be called that, was marked by ill-feeling and dissent from start to finish. Matt Wright was engaged by AMC in 1938 as development engineer responsible for racing engines, but company director D. H. Heather hired Joe Craig to do the same job, in the hope that some of his magic with Nortons would rub off on AJS. Harry Collier would have nothing to do with Craig, and the design and drawing of the new racer, reduced to a parallel twin from a triple, was said to be done by Vic Webb with the help of Phil Irving, and drawings for a complete supercharged machine had been completed when the F.I.M. announced, at its Paris congress late in November 1946, that superchargers would not be allowed in racing after 1946.

Matt Wright remained development engineer at AJS throughout this time. He was landed with an engine which needed a serious rethink to correct the high inertia and low compression ratio normal for a supercharged engine. A new cylinder-head was designed and some flywheel effect was built into the crankshaft. A fast and handsome racing motorcycle was ready for the 1947 season, but the engine became one of the less reliable in Grand Prix racing. A mass of fine fins on the cylinder head of the flat twin led to the new AJS being nicknamed "the Porcupine", a term more commonly used than the official type title of E90.

AJS were unlucky to be probably the company most badly affected by the ban on superchargers. Norton had never considered them. Velocette had abandoned their prototype "Roarer", a supercharged parallel twin that was not raced in 1939 after it was tried in TT practice, and Velocette were happy to revive their successful singles. On the continent Moto Guzzi and Benelli had excellent unsupercharged racing motorcycles, and Gilera, who were champions of Europe in 1939 with a team of massive blown four-cylinder machines, had a handy air-cooled four on the drawing board which was successfully translated into an unsupercharged racer by the middle of 1947. Germany was excluded from the FIM and races outside Germany until 1951; there were numerous road race courses and tracks in Germany and plenty of supercharged BMWs, NSUs and DKWs to be

The great Italian, Omobono Tenni, started racing at the same time as Les and was the mainstay of the Moto Guzzi team before the war. He is here at Berne after winning the 500cc Swiss Grand Prix in 1947, with the Swiss Guzzi agent.

raced around them by private and factory riders, so they enjoyed their sport and had time to prepare for their return to the international scene.

The Porcupine was not ready for test riding in 1946. Jock West took a prewar supercharged AJS Vee four to the Albi Grand Prix in France to keep his hand in, but there was nothing for Les to race when he left the RAF for AJS later in the year. At his own suggestion, Les worked on a standard pushrod AJS to convert it into an ultra-light hillclimb and short circuit machine, and later produced an even lighter Matchless version, whose acceleration was enough to make it monowheel away from hillclimb starts. But for a man devoted to speed and competition, 1946 was an empty season.

———❖———

Thanks to the F.I.M., there was no time left to test the machines between completion of two AJS "porcupine" twins and the start of TT practice at the end of May, 1947. Jock West, who was both works rider and AJS team manager, briefly rode one on a road near the factory, but then it was off to the Isle of Man. In practice Jock West had a stomach-churning

moment when one of the alloy handlebars broke at Kirchmichael, leaving the throttle twist grip dangling in the air as he sped toward the village. He managed to turn the twistgrip back against the fuel tank and loyally pretended it was "just one of those things" when he got back to Douglas. Les fared even worse, lacerating his hand in a fall at Signpost corner. Several of the top riders had practice falls, including Artie Bell, Les Archer junior, Kenneth Bills and Freddie Frith, whose front brake on his works Guzzi locked at Ballacraine, causing shoulder injuries that put him out of the TT and the rest of the international season. It is hard to imagine how much rougher and narrower the roads round the course were then, compared to today.

Jock West looked good and rode fast in practice, but had serious trouble starting the bike on race day. After over a minute he got away, only to suffer clutch slip and achieve a lap time of 84.19 minutes compared to the leader, Harold Daniell's first lap of 27.17 minutes. Somehow, Jock's clutch recovered and he made the fastest lap of any rider on the fourth lap, averaging 83.6 mph. He kept up this level of speed to the end of the race, showing that the 'Porcupine' had winning potential. Running fourth at the end of the first lap, Les fell off at Glen

The start of a German national championship race. All the most successful German racers from before the war came back to do fierce battle on factory BMWs and NSUs or their own private machines. Here at Solitude, left to right, are George Meier, BMW, Heiner Fleischman, N.S.U., and L.Kraus, B.M.W. These bikes are all supercharged.

Helen, and recovered to sixth place. On the last lap his chain broke at Governor's bridge and Les pushed in to ninth place. What he said at the finish was not recorded, but being well taught in the school of hard knocks, he probably found something to laugh about.

It must have been very frustrating to see Norton dominate the TT and European Grand Prix races in 1947, with the machines the factory had built for the 1938 TT races, for a team which was struggling to get a good finish on a brand new design. Artie Bell had a cracking season, winning the Dutch, and the Ulster races, and coming second in the Senior TT and the Swiss Grand Prix with wins in major non-championship events like the North West 200. At the Ulster Grand Prix in August the AJS team made a respectable showing, Jock West and Ted Frend finishing third and fifth after two and three quarter hours of racing. Les started but did not finish the race.

In September '47 Les returned to prewar form and to one of his favourite circuits, Cadwell. Riding his lightweight pushrod Matchless, Les rode hard and fast, setting a new 500cc lap record which remained unbroken until 1950. Then in October the AJS twin

won its first race, a minor race at the airfield circuit at Dunholme. Ted Frend and Les took off and got well ahead. "We had a really good scrap, out in front, until Les' magneto packed up." Ted Frend was a very good rider, who managed to fit Grand Prix races in between his own sheet metal business when it was convenient and often finished in one of the first three places.

It had been a rocky start for the new twin but it had much improved since its first appearance. Matt Wright had raised the engine's power from a poor 29bhp on the first test bed run to 37bhp. This unimpressive figure was in fact close to the power of the factory Nortons, which like AJS were running on "pool" petrol with an octane rating in the low 70s, and the Porcupine was a useful 20 to 25lb lighter. Ted Frend and Les found the handling acceptable for their grass track experience had prepared them for wobbles and looseness on the road. The main handicap to sorting out remaining problems was the company's determination to stick to their mass-production suppliers of carburettors and magnetos for racing, and if a part broke, to replace it without a thorough study of why it went wrong. Nevertheless, the team felt they had a potential winner and looked forward to success.

A fascinating shot of the 1946 "Ulster Road Race", unfortunately taken from a poor print. On the starting grid number 9 is Rex McCandless with his advanced Triumph-engined special, with the frame that was taken on by Norton for the 1950 "featherbed" racers. Others are No.11, Artie Bell, No.3, Les Graham, Norton, No.14, Ernie Lyons, prototype Triumph Grand Prix. None of these riders finished.

Nello Pagani raced for Moto Guzzi before the war, winning several European Grands Prix on the supercharged 250cc single in 1939. He rode the hefty supercharged Gilera seen here in several races in 1946 and 1947.

Les racing at Cadwell Park on the lightweight special Matchless, whose construction kept him busy while the works 500cc racer was under construction. He set a new lap record at Cadwell.

Omobono Tenni circulating the warm-up area before practice for the 1948 TT. He rides the Guzzi V-twin which was the fastest Italian machine until Gilera got their post-war four-cylinder racer going properly. He looks untypically unhappy, perhaps because of weather conditions.

1948 – A Year of Frustration

The programme of major international races that was established before the war also set the programme for 1948. First the Swiss GP, then the TT, the Dutch, the Belgian, and the Ulster Grands Prix and lastly the Grand Prix des Nations, as the Italian Grand Prix was called. In 1950 the Spanish Grand Prix was added. Minor international races offering good start money and either fancy trophies or more welcome cash as prizes attracted riders from far afield, including a growing number of Australian, New Zealand and South African riders, most of them very good. A group calling themselves "The Continental

Circus", of mostly English-speaking riders, travelled together to their favourite races, camping in simple tents and elderly vans, while showing great appreciation of what their host location had to offer in food, drink and society. Many British riders coming from a land of shortages and rationing were surprised at the good things that seemed readily available in the shops and cafes of France and Italy, countries far worse battered by the war than Britain.

The men who were employed to race for manufacturers were practically all relatively mature

Artie Bell, the most successful Northern Irish rider until serious injury in 1950 ended his career. Bell was a most popular Norton rider, who directed a thriving business as well as racing professionally. He is on one of the long-serving 1938 works Nortons at Quarter Bridge during the 1948 TT.

men in their mid-thirties, who had raced before 1939. Les, for example, was 37, but no one thought for a moment that this was anything approaching too old. The works teams of Great Britain and Italy, the only countries with factory teams at this time, were all around this age. Norton fielded a splendid team of Harold Daniell, Artie Bell and Johnnie Lockett. The AJS team were Jock West, Les Graham and Ted Frend; Velocette, fielding 350cc machines only, had Freddie Frith, Bob Foster, David Whitworth and Ken Bills in their team. Gilera ran a varying team based on Pagani and Artesiani on the new four cylinder machines. The Moto Guzzi team was led by the phenomenal Omobono Tenni, backed by Enrico Lorenzetti in 500cc races, and a host of riders who seemed to take turns in 250cc races. The Benelli concern has to be included, for their rider Ambrosini was a superb racer, and similar to Tenni in skill and personality.

AJS gave the Swiss Grand Prix, run on May 15, a miss, except for a 350 entry for Les which produced a sixth place. Besides preparing the 500cc twins for Jock West, Les and Ted Frend to ride in the Senior TT in June, AJS had launched a new 350cc racing model for sale to the private owner. This was designated the 7R and used a chain-driven single OHC engine, in a

cradle frame virtually copied from the Porcupine. It was a good-looking machine, (though one suspects that any racing motorcycle is good-looking to the enthusiast,) and it filled a gap in availability of modern racers. Launched early in 1948, it sold very well and 23 were entered for the Junior TT, including three for the AJS team. Four more were entered in the Senior race. Some people, certainly not their owners, patronisingly called the 7R the "Boy Racer." It was probably the most popular "over-the-counter" racer post-war until the two-stroke revolution.

The 1948 TT was a huge success for the 7R. In the Junior TT Maurice Cann finished fourth behind the works Velocettes of Frith and Foster, and Johnnie Lockett's works Norton. In the Senior TT G. G. Murdoch finished an astonishing fourth on the private 350cc AJS, on which he had come in 37th in the Junior. We don't know why he finished so low in the Junior, a fall or mechanical problem, no doubt, but after his impressive Senior finish he never rode in the TT again.

It was a dismal TT for the AJS factory team. In the Junior Ted Frend fell at Glen Helen, Les toiled up from 12th on lap one to 7th at the finish, and Jock West finished 13th. The Senior was worse. Omobono

Tenni again, this time leading the 1948 TT. His style was dashing, to say the least and suggested that he was a fearless rider, in the literal sense.

Tenni took the works Moto Guzzi into a 29 second lead on lap one, on a spectacular ride which included the "longest ever" speed wobble seen on Bray Hill, with Les Graham in hot but distant pursuit. Jock West also shocked the spectators, by passing two riders on the way down Bray Hill, a very rare manoeuvre. Not one of the three AJS twins finished, two retiring with mechanical failure, one from damage to Jock West's throttle cable by a malevolent bird. From his lead of 65 seconds ahead of Artie Bell, Tenni dropped back to ninth place with a combination of spark plug and fuel problems, leaving Artie to win from Bill Doran on a private Norton.

The Dutch TT, a fortnight after the Senior TT, was a complete wipe-out for Les. Only one AJS was entered in the 350 race, ridden by Ted Frend, who crashed heavily on the last lap after a long tussle for third place with Eric Briggs on a Norton. Jock West and Les started the 500 race in company with Bell and Daniell, five Gileras, led by Masserini on one of the new four cylinder machines, four Guzzis and a good supporting field which included two private BMWs and a Sarolea. Absent was the Guzzi rider, Tenni, who was in Berne practicing for the motorcycle races that took place during the week of the Swiss car Grand Prix in Berne. On July 1st Tenni crashed fatally on a

bend in the forest section of the course. Italy lost and mourned one of the world's finest riders. On the same day Achille Varzi crashed his Alfa Romeo 158 Grand Prix car on the same circuit and was killed. Varzi had ridden with success on the Isle of Man between 1924 and 1930, mainly on Sunbeams, finishing seventh in the 1926 Senior. His reserved and dignified persona was practically the opposite of Tenni's fearless enthusiasm.

Returning to Holland, Les did not even complete the first lap before a punctured float chamber put him out of the race. Once again Jock West kept going to take 3rd place. One week later, on the fast and beautiful Spa circuit on which the Belgian Grand Prix took place, Jock's magic worked again, and he finished a close second to Johnnie Lockett's Norton. "MotorCycling" magazine injected human interest into their dramatic report of the start of the 500cc race:

"Away they go. It is almost a perfect start with no one left on the grid. In the first mile or so Bell leads Frith and Daniell, but, by Malmedy, Daniell and Lockett occupy second and third place. Nortons one, two and three again? Wait, we have reckoned without one whose share of good fortune in post-war events has

The AJS factory team with the 1948 Porcupine during testing. Left to right: Ted Frend, Jock West, Fred Clarke (Development Engineer,) and Les. Note the straight-through exhaust pipes.

The 1948 "Porcupines" in the racing department of the AJS factory. The carburettor and curved inlet tract drawing air from under the tank can be seen.

not been more than a crumb. He is R. L. Graham. On the swerves between Malmedy and Stavelot he "Cadwells" his way through the bunch and gets on Daniell's tail. Before Francorchamps he leads, and he completes Lap 1 with Lockett a second in the rear."

With what must have been equal "Cadwelling", Jock West surged past all three Nortons, from 5th to 2nd place behind Les. Both riders averaged 93mph on this second lap, and Les improved on this on the third lap to make the fastest lap of the day. Then Les' engine started to misfire, badly enough to need a pit stop for new plugs, which lost him eight places. Jock West maintained his second place to the finish, even closing on the final winner, Johnnie Lockett. Les only managed seventh place in the 350cc Belgian GP, behind G.G.Murdoch who had came fourth in the Junior TT on the same 7R AJS. So far, Les had nothing to celebrate as works rider for AJS, except fastest lap in the Belgian Grand Prix.

The last international Grand Prix in 1948 with riders from British factories was the Ulster Grand Prix, the twentieth to be held on the Clady circuit. A certain amount of rain was usual for the Ulster. In his book about the Ulster series, G. S. Davison, who had raced in the 1924 event and watched almost every other, described the special quality of the rain in 1948 in loving detail.

"It was one of those days which started badly and rapidly grew worse. In the early morning it was drizzling; by 11am it was raining heavily and by the starting time, noon, it was lashing with rain and blowing almost a hurricane. Some idea of the wind can be gathered from the fact that when I was taking photographs of the start I had to get an official to hold on to me to prevent me from being blown into the

path of the competitors. It was the sort of rain-storm that normally wears itself out in a few minutes; on the Clady circuit that day it covered the whole four hour period of the race." It was agreed by enthusiasts with a long memory that the rain surpassed even that of the 1923 Senior TT, when several soaked riders expressed relief when their machines broke down before the end.

The 250cc, 350cc and 500cc races were run at the same time, with a short interval between the starts of each class. Norton entered the usual team of Daniell, Bell and Lockett, while AJS entered Jock West, Les and Ted Frend. Guzzi and Velocette also entered teams, and the number of riders who splashed off at the start of the Senior class of the Ulster GP was 28. In the continuing downpour water affected many engines including the entire AJS team, and Jock West had to retire after his usual good start. By lap twelve of the fifteen only twelve riders of the twenty-eight who started were in the running, and a battle had developed for the lead between Lorenzetti, Bell, Lockett and Les. On lap 11 Lorenzetti slipped in front of Bell and Lockett, and Bell's effort to regain the lead finished with a tyre-destroying collision with the bank at Clady corner.

On his first visit to Ulster, in very un-mediterranean weather, Lorenzetti increased his lead to finish 19 seconds ahead of Lockett and five minutes ahead of Les, who had ridden his spluttering AJS with determination. There were no other finishers as the surviving nine stragglers were so far behind on lap 12 that they had been flagged off.

The last international Grand Prix, the Italian, at Faenza, was not contested by British manufacturers. Fergus Anderson, a strong-minded Scotsman and protagonist

1948 SHELSLEY WALSH
INTERNATIONAL HILL CLIMB
NEW MOTOR CYCLE RECORD 38.87 Secs
R. L. Graham, 498 c.c. MATCHLESS

THE MOTOR CYCLE
Photograph.

The lightweight Matchless at Shelsey Walsh in 1948, where Les set a new record for motorcycles. He was quicker off the mark than most of his competitors in road races as well.

of riders' rights, was there as a member of the Guzzi team, five of which faced five Gileras. Masserini gave the new four cylinder Gilera a historic first win.

In contrast to the tensions and disappointments of the Grand Prix season, Les entered his sprint AJS 350 and Matchless 500 in the Autumn hillclimb at Shelsey Walsh. This was in two parts: the open competition between all comers, and a closed team event between three Midland Auto Club cars and three BMCRC motorcycles. Raymond Mays, Bob Gerard and Dennis Poore drove the cars, Freddie Frith, Harold Daniell and Les rode the motorcycles.

Only a thousand yards long, Shelsey requires inch-perfect negotiation to achieve a respectable time, together with powerful acceleration. Les demonstrated both of these and set new record times in both 350cc and 500cc classes. In the team match he muffed a gear change on the Matchless and took one and a half seconds longer than his record time of 38.87 seconds. (The hill record was 37.37, set in 1937 by Raymond Mays on his ERA.) Fastest motorcyclist of the day was Frith on a Triumph with

38.69, but as this was in the closed team event it was not recognised as a hill record.

In his participation in Shelsey Les met and became friends with several men involved with motor racing at a high level, drivers and entrants. Raymond Mays was a good friend and Les was interested to hear about progress with the BRM Grand Prix car, which was May's main business.

AJS entered the usual team of three in two home events at the end of the season - Dunholme and the Silverstone BMCRC 100 miles Grand Prix. Les won both races, with Ted Frend behind him. Jock West was fourth at Dunholme and third at Silverstone. In five major international races Les retired from two with mechanical breakdowns and in the three that he finished he was deprived of a higher place by either electrical or carburettor trouble. With the exception of Omobono Tenni, there was no one faster while the machine ran well. In the course of the year he clearly emerged as a rider of the very top class, but an unlucky one. He must have asked himself more than once: "Will AJS ever provide a reliable engine?"

Les Graham in tigerish mode in practice for the Silverstone Autumn "Grand Prix". Les has found a strange helmet for the occasion. He won the race with Ted on a second Porcupine close behind.

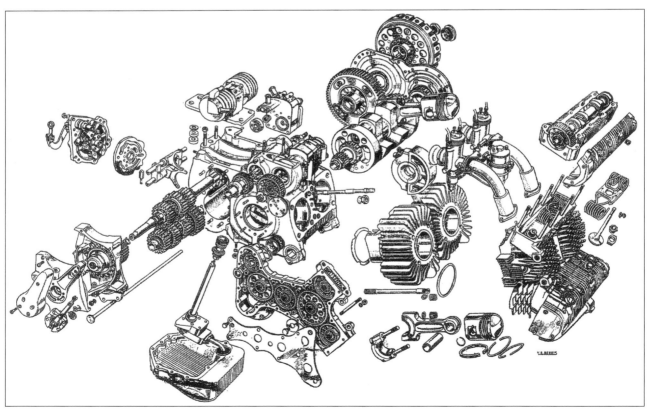

An "exploded" view of the E90 AJS engine. It had gear-driven overhead camshafts and a gear-driven gearbox. The spiky cooling fins that gave the engine its title of "Porcupine" are on the cam boxes. The engine was not as successful as it should have been, though the 1949 World's Championship was no small success. Unreliability for all kinds of reasons was its bugbear.

The 1949 Porcupine had repositioned carburettors with the intakes out in the fresh air and the float chambers attached to the frame. Ted Frend thought this was not a good idea as the frame took up engine vibration.

1949: The Competition

At the end of the 1948 racing season, it seemed that the galaxy of stars who had made British enthusiasts proud in 1938 and 1939 would shine for ever. Harold Daniell and Johnnie Lockett still represented Norton, with Artie Bell; Freddie Frith, Ernie Lyons and Bob Foster rode the works Velocettes, and Jock West led a team which included Les Graham and Ted Frend – the latter two experienced prewar riders whose ability was only fully recognised after the war.

But in 1949 new riders appeared who would change the balance and challenge the established stars. Among these were Reg Armstrong from Dublin, Dickie Dale, Sid Lawton, Cecil Sandford, the Australian Harry Hinton and a quiet young man who worked in Norton's competition department, Geoff Duke. In the next two years more good riders graduated to international racing, including the outstanding Commonwealth trio of Rod Coleman, Ken Kavanagh and Ray Amm. The outlook for strong manufacturers teams in the future was good. Was the machinery equally good?

Unlike AJS with new E90 Porcupine and 7R, development of racing engines and frames at Norton and Velocette had barely moved since the end of the war. Velocette's profits were limited after the war by the difficulty of getting raw materials for motorcycles that were wanted, and by the high development costs and disappointing sales of motorcycles that people did not want – specifically the silent LE luxury model. Although the racing machines for 1949 were powered by new double overhead camshaft engines, Velocette's international wins were the products of Freddie Frith's flawless riding, not technical development. After serious consideration of a four cylinder racing engine in 1950, Velocette continued to supply a few racing machines to selected riders and sponsors, but in 1952 they finally closed down their racing department.

Norton were not much better off in spite of a much larger turnover. The motorcycles raced by the factory team in 1949 were the same actual machines built for the 1938 TT, that Norton entered for international races in 1946, 47 and 48. A new front fork which

The Moto Guzzi "bicilindrica" in 1949 form. The fuel tank on the Guzzi twin was altered almost every year from 1947, while the single OHC engine remained almost unchanged. Apart from the famous engine, with its twisting exhausts and inlet pipes, notable features were the neat leading link front suspension, and the under-engine rear suspension damper.

achieved a more vertical angle was introduced by Joe Craig early in 1949 in the belief that steering would be improved, but all the works riders disliked it and the old type was refitted. Norton's chief advantage was reliability, and when the speeding AJS and Velocettes faltered, there were always Nortons ready to take their place. This was hardly progress, and Norton, like Velocette, hoped to have a winning four cylinder engine before it was too late.

Joe Craig asked Raymond Mays to take on design of such an engine alongside his development of the BRM 16 cylinder Grand Prix car, not realising that the BRM project was wallowing in problems of new technology and bad management.

A studio picture of the air-cooled Gilera four. It was a handsome and effective machine that inspired the design of many other cross-frame fours, from Benelli to Vostock to a few enterprising shed-built specials. The friction shock-absorbers for the rear suspension and the large "rocking" gearchange pedal are clearly visible.

Norton's racing future was assured not by the engineers at BRM but by Rex McCandless, an untrained engineer (like Leonardo da Vinci) who built and tested the creations of his unconventional mind. These included aircraft, a four-wheel drive racing car and a lightweight twin tube frame for motorcycles, thoroughly developed to give good roadholding and a low profile. Artie Bell, later Rex's business partner and also an Ulster man, saw the potential benefit of this frame to Norton, and with difficulty persuaded Joe Craig to listen to McCandless, a man as fiery and unbending as Joe himself.

As for AJS, they had the fastest 500cc racer with the Porcupine twin, and a 350cc racer at least as fast as its competitors. The problem with the company was that Jock West and the engineers of the racing department were on a tight rein held by Donald Heather and the board of AJS, particularly as far as components were concerned. The board seemed to regard each racing breakdown as an isolated bit of bad luck, and would not hear of the magnetos, carburettors or suspension units supplied by their faithful mass production sources, Lucas, Amal and Girling, being redesigned or even replaced by other manufacturers.

When Rod Coleman joined the AJS factory team late in 1951 he was surprised to experience the same problems of unreliable magnetos and uneven carburation he knew that the early Porcupines had suffered from. These were dangerous faults, as the engine would practically cut out in a bend, then fire up with full power again

Too handsome to illustrate only once, here is the 1949 Gilera again, in the paddock at the Ulster Grand Prix. Nello Pagani as usual, looks serious, everyone else has found something interesting to study on these exotic machines. *FoTTofinders*

while the machine was still banked over. Most AJS team riders fell or nearly fell at one time or another when this happened. Matt Wright did his level best to stop the erratic fuel feed by going to two and even three float chambers, and swapping the carburettor location to take air from under the fuel tank to out in the airstream. Probably caused by fuel surge on faster corners, the resulting misfire was never fully cured. But thanks to Matt's work on cams and cylinder heads, the porcupine developed a healthy 50 brake horsepower at the start of the 1949 season, while it was one of the lightest 500cc machines in competition.

Moto Guzzi was by far the largest Italian motorcycle manufacturer throughout the 1940s and 50s. The racing Guzzi Vee twin first appeared in 1933 and probably was at its most competitive between 1935 and 1938. Its performance in the 1948 TT showed what a well-handling and fast machine it was, capable of dealing safely with the ferocious style of Tenni, but it was neither first or second in any other Grand Prix in 1949, although it was reliable. It was slower than the Porcupine and the new Gilera in a straight line, but its other virtues were to produce more wins before it was pensioned off in 1952. In the Lightweight 250cc class Moto Guzzi developed very effective single cylinder machines, the Albatross and the Gambalunghino, which were light and handled well and were ridden by a host of factory and private riders. In the 1948 250cc Swiss Grand Prix nine Moto Guzzis were among the ten finishers, and in 1949 ten Moto Guzzis were among the first twelve

finishers. A well run company with an exceptional competition department, Moto Guzzi was an example to companies where poor communication between managers and engineers was a normal state of affairs.

In strong contrast to Guzzi was the Italian manufacturer who actually won the 1948 Swiss Grand Prix and was second in 1949 - Benelli. Like Moto Guzzi it was a well-run family firm, but pre-war it had never matched the size of Guzzi, and while Guzzi survived the war with a thriving business, Benelli was ravaged by German destruction and the removal of much of their manufacturing machinery to Germany. Amazingly, with only two surviving racing machines and the determination of the gifted Dario Ambrosini, Benelli regularly bested Moto Guzzi in 1948 and 1949 in many races. In 1950 Ambrosini was a popular 250cc World Champion.

Benelli did not race a 500cc machine after the war, but Ambrosini entered several 350cc races when the rules allowed it and had little trouble keeping up with the leaders. However, the most successful Italian manufacturer in the 500cc class was Gilera. Gilera, like Guzzi, survived the war in good condition, and work on an unsupercharged four cylinder engine was already under way in 1946 by the engineer Piero Remor and Giuseppe Gilera.

Gilera re-entered competition with a strong team of riders. Until the new four cylinder racer was ready, the works team, led by Masserini, Pagani and Bandirola,

Three top-flight British riders; from left to right, Maurice Cann, versatile rider and a capable engineer, Freddie Frith, the Geoff Duke of the thirties and still a superb rider until 1950, and Les Graham. They are at the Ulster Grand Prix, 1949, where Cann won the 250 race, Frith won the 350 race and Les won the 500 race. *FoTTofinders*

Harold Daniell after winning the 1949 Senior TT. To his left are Gilbert Smith, Norton Chairman, Mrs Daniell and Steve Lancefield, Harold's brother-in-law and supporter/sponsor.

rode Gilera single cylinder "Saturno" machines. These were robust motorcycles, on sale to the public as sports or touring machines, while a competition model with lightweight frame and modified engine was good enough to beat the factory Guzzi twins in a major national race early in 1947 at San Remo.

When the new Gilera "four" first raced in 1948 it suffered from magneto and lubrication problems. The pressed steel forks and rear swing arm also caused handling problems, to the degree that Pagani withdrew from his first race on the four declaring the motorcycle "unrideable". This enraged designer Piero Remor, and morale was low until one of the new machines won the 1948 "Grand Prix des Nations" or Italian Grand Prix, ridden by Masserini, (with no British factory competition.) Those who were not directly involved in arguments with Remor could see that the "Quattro" had great potential.

Italy faced the 1949 season with the same hopes and worries as Britain: she had a wealth of excellent experienced riders capable of producing a performance of the standard of Britain's best. There were also plenty of good newcomers, some making their start on the many different ultra-lightweight 125cc machines with which Italy dominated that class of racing. Most of her racing machines were either developments of pre-war models or the pre-war models themselves, but manufacturers engaged in racing knew that they needed new designs to stay competitive in the future. The Italians seemed to have the money and will to do this. The outlook for the 1949 Grand Prix season was for some hard, close racing.

Les Graham working hard to catch Geoff Duke at Haddenham, after running wide at a corner.

Championship Year – Part One

The international racing year of 1949 opened with an announcement by the Federation International Motorcycliste that it would organize a World's Championship for riders and manufacturers as part of the European Grand Prix programme. This was a step up from the European Championships run in 1938 and 1939, and won by Georg Meier (BMW) and Dorino Serafini (Gilera) respectively. The pre-war Championship had included the 500cc class only; the new series was to include Ultra-Lightweight (125cc,) Lightweight (250cc,) 350cc solo, 500cc solo and 500cc sidecar classes.

The inclusion of the two lightweight classes was welcomed by Italy, but her riders and fans were not happy about the TT Races being among the six qualifying events. A few top Italian riders had

the will and the money or backing to participate over the years, and were among the best to ride on the Isle of Man, but most riders and factories understandably avoided it for reasons of expense and lack of knowledge of the long course. But the FIM, chaired this year by Great Britain, had made its mind up and included the Isle of Man TT, the Swiss GP, the Dutch TT, the Belgian GP, the Ulster GP and the Italian GP in the contest.

Another worry of some riders and organisers was that the supervision of, and interference with, major races by the FIM would reduce the relaxed and friendly atmosphere of these events. They were proved right by some high-handed actions in the years to come. Generally, though, it was thought that the World's Championship would raise public interest in motorcycles and encourage

Freddie Frith, stylish and in control at Ballough Bridge during his winning 1949 Junior TT ride.

Geoff Duke hangs on to the lead at Haddenham on his "dope fuelled" Norton. Note spanner in boot for running repairs and gappy leathers that inspired him to "invent" the one-piece riding suit.

manufacturers to try harder to produce winning machines.

No one could accuse AJS of failing to try hard. The racing department had done its best to improve the reliability as well as the power of both the 350cc and the 500cc contenders, though the same components that had given so much trouble were unaltered. An interesting change was the repositioning of the carburettor intakes from their enclosed site under the tank to the airflow outside. An early start to the British racing season gave an opportunity to test the changes before the TT.

First event was on April 3rd at Haddenham, a narrow airfield perimeter course which twisted round the runways and parked Halifax bombers. AJS entered only one rider, Les, in the 350cc race, which turned out to be as much a test of his skill as of the machine. Of the heats, one was won by Les, the other by Geoff Duke on his own short-circuit Norton, on petrol/benzol fuel. Coming together in the final, Les took off ahead of Geoff, but Geoff stuck to his tail and as soon as Les went wide at a bend, leaving the road and touching a straw bale, Geoff took the lead and held it to the finish. In his book "Pursuit of Perfection", Geoff recalls feeling nervous of Les' reaction to being beaten by a novice. He had met Les at the AJS factory when considering employment at Plumstead in 1948, and although Les was very welcoming, he was disparaging of Geoff's hopes of entering the Manx Grand Prix while working for a manufacturer with a racing department. Geoff turned to Norton for employment as road racing was his great ambition.

But this was water under the bridge, and at the finish at Haddenham Les drew alongside Duke, thumped him on the back, shook his hand and

gave him warm congratulations. This was his normal ebullient reaction to someone's excellent performance, specially if the rider was a newcomer. Next race was Anstey; Duke was not there and Les won the 350cc race quite comfortably from his old Wallasey friend Ken Dixon, and the 500cc race not so comfortably from Bob Foster on a Triumph. Les rode his lightweight Matchless single in this race.

The next event on April 18, was at the fast three mile course that surrounded Blandford army camp. Les had a Porcupine twin and a 7R for the races and Norton entered Harold Daniell and Johnnie Lockett on 350cc bikes destined for the TT. Geoff Duke was there with his 350cc "dope-fuelled" Norton. Les and Duke each won their heat for the 350 race, but this time in the final Les kept on the track and finished in front of Geoff. On his own machine, Geoff beat the works Nortons of Daniell and Lockett, and although their Nortons were handicapped by running on "Pool" petrol rather than "dope," the extraordinary ability of Duke was clear to everyone at Blandford. Les might have hoped for an easy win on the only works machine in the 500cc race, but Bob Foster, as he had often done before, gave him a very hard race to finish half a second behind him in the 500cc final.

At the beginning of May the Continental Circus gathered to race at Floreffe, in Belgium. The itinerent riders pitched camp in a handy wood close to the circuit, where they were joined by Les Graham, Freddie Frith, Kenneth Bills and Dario Ambrosini who were taking a busman's holiday, with AJS, Velocette and Benelli machines in tow. This group, particularly Les and Ambrosini, enjoyed anything resembling a party and must have been welcomed in spite of being

"The descent of Bray Hill could make me gulp" Les once said. He looks fully in control in the 1949 Senior TT.

The start of a long push. Les toils up Cronk-ny-Mona after breaking down while in the lead of the 1949 TT.

certain winners. So it turned out, with Ambrosini winning the 250cc race, and Les the 350cc and 500cc races. Frith was a surprising 30 seconds behind Les in the 350 race, hotly pursued by Ambrosini, whose 250 finished ahead of thirteen 350s, mostly Velocettes. Eric Oliver duly won the sidecar race. The standard of crowd control in Belgian races at that time was poor, and some riders could not get used to a sort of Mexican Wave of spectators who stepped off the pavement to look for the next rider, then stepped back before the rider passed by. After the races, most of the riders invited themselves to a party which was in full swing in the next village to Floreffe, where they were warmly welcomed, some having trouble finding their tents afterwards.

The final pre-TT event for AJS was Eppynt, the wild and narrow "Welsh TT". This dangerous 5.2 mile course wound through the Mynydd Eppynt mountains and was a challenge to racers and a joy to spectators. Les won both Junior and Senior finals on the same 350cc AJS.

On May 31st the "King Orrie", pride of the Isle of Man Steam Packet fleet, landed at Douglas crammed with spectators, borough engineers over for a conference, and the racing machines and personnel of the AJS and Norton teams.

AJS were reported to have emptied two large truckloads of machines and parts onto the boat at Liverpool, ("drive on" was not a term known to ferry companies in 1949.)

Until 2004 every TT was organised by the Auto Cycle Union - the ACU - and the ACU withstood many brickbats and a few compliments to present a vast and complex racing event on the Isle of Man for the best part of a hundred years. The ACU recruited the scrutineers and marshals needed for the race, bashed every rider's helmet to make sure it was sound and allocated numbers to riders as they thought best. Number 1 in the Junior and Senior races was allocated to the previous year's winner; number 13 was not allocated at all. Riders had and still have preferences for their place in the starting order, but the fastest riders generally prefer to be ahead of the bulk of riders for obvious reasons. The ACU remained tight-lipped about the starting order until programmes had been printed and distributed - about a week after practice began. When the numbers were given out most of the fastest riders had numbers within the first half the seventy allocated. Only Artie Bell was down at 69 on his Junior Norton, but in the Senior, as last year's winner, he was number 1. Frith, riding works 350 and 500 Velocettes, was number 1 in the Junior, and 29 in the Senior.

Les is joined by Jock West on the Glencrutchery road as he approaches the finish.

Practice was the usual mixture of surprises, mishaps, rain and high speed from the best factory riders. Bell, Les and Ted Frend were the three fastest seniors, at over or just under 87mph; Les, Ernie Lyons and Reg Armstrong were the three fastest Juniors. One assumes that Frith was not in a hurry as his average for the actual race was faster than Les' fastest practice lap. The "experts" in the motorcycling press admitted to being unable to choose a winner but were confident that in both Junior and Senior races he would be one of Graham, Frith, Foster, Bell or Daniell.

The 1949 Junior TT was a sad disappointment for AJS and its leading riders, Les and Bill Doran. This pair led at the end of lap one from Frith, only for Les to stop on lap two to attempt clutch adjustments which were not successful. Doran kept ahead of Frith and led laps two, three, four, five and six, keeping a ten to twenty second lead. Halfway round the last lap Doran's gearbox gave up, so Frith won at an average of 83.15 mph from Lyons, Bell, Daniell and the surviving works AJS ridden by Reg Armstrong. Ernie Lyons was well on his way on an extra lap

before he realised he was on his own. He was very kind about the official who failed to show him the finishing flag.

Frith made fastest lap at 84.23mph. Frith was a smooth, stylish and fast rider, considered by some to be the best rider of the late 30s and 40s. All three Nortons finished and won the Manufacturers Team prize, while more private 7R AJS finished than any other single make.

The Senior was one of the dramatic TT races of all time. Bell, Les Graham, Harold Daniell, Ted Frend, Bob Foster, Frith and Bill Doran had the starting numbers 1, 4, 14, 15, 27, 29 and 32, giving all the top riders a chance of actually seeing each other during the race. Bell started alone as number 1, the rest of the field started in twos at 20 second intervals. Les and Ted Frend completed lap one in exactly the same time, a new postwar record, and dead-heated for the lead – 11 seconds ahead of Daniell – although Frend was five minutes behind Les on the road due to his start number. Similarly Bill Doran and Johnnie Lockett tied for fifth place with a lap 20 seconds slower than the leaders.

The finish. A tired Les scoots over the line with Jock West. In the background scouts put on an impromptu naval display.

On lap two Bob Foster forced his Guzzi Vee-twin round 37 seconds faster than his first lap and caught Les and Ted on time, to provide an amazing triple dead heat for the lead. Bob lapped 29 seconds faster than Omobono's hair-raising record lap in 1948, helped by a little development of the Guzzi twin and the usual road improvements. His riding was as fearless as that of the late Italian. The Nortons held fourth, sixth and seventh places, slowly but surely falling behind the leading trio.

On lap three, where skill and precision in slowing for the refuelling stop could save seconds over untidy riders, Foster took over the lead from what was now a trio of Porcupines, the fastest Ted Frend, now 12 seconds ahead of Les.

Bob Foster steadily increased his lead over the AJS team in laps four and five; Ted Frend had a high speed crash at Glen Helen on the fifth lap which left him shaken but uninjured and Foster led Les by nearly one minute. But it was Foster's turn for bad luck when his clutch gave out at Sulby. Les and Foster were very good friends, and when Bob retired in 1951 he ran Les' pits with Edna Graham

and the occasional help of Les' young nephew, Jim. His retirement left Les in the lead with over a minute and a half in hand over Daniell.

Into the last lap sped Les, showing no sign of easing off. The radio commentator at Greg-ny-Baa watched him sweeping through the corner toward Hilberry, but the next commentator, at Cronk-ny-Mona, announced that Les had appeared on his feet, pushing his machine. He assumed Les had run out of fuel, but in fact once again the magneto had failed when the armature drive shaft sheared. Les pushed and coasted roughly two miles, encouraged by Jock West who walked with him, along the last stretch to the pits, to finish twelve minutes behind the winner.

After the race and the commiserations of other riders, Les said he was more sorry for Bob Foster, who led for three laps increasing his lead before breaking down. Typically, with a wish to see a positive side to events, Les said that his retirement highlighted a magneto fault which was now identified and curable. He also said he never wanted to push up Cronk-ny-Mona again.

1949 Ulster Grand Prix. Giving spectators the full volume of the 500cc Porcupine's exhaust, Les changes down for a bend on the Clady circuit. *FoTTofinders*

Championship Year – Part Two

In the early summer of 1949 Les Graham was on top of his form as a racing motorcyclist. It was a profession that he relished at the age of 38 every bit as much as he had at 25, and he was as ready to ride near the ragged edge of his talent as he ever had been. He was very fast away from the starting grid on any machine. Both of the motorcycles raced by the factory, the 350cc 7R and the 500cc E90 Porcupine, appeared to be faster than their competitors. However, one could be sure that the Italians had not been asleep, and the best machines were capable of breaking down.

Two weeks after the Senior TT came the first of the continental Grands Prix to count for the new World Championship - the Swiss Grand Prix. The Dutch and Belgian Grands Prix were to be on the two following weekends.

Bremgarten, the Swiss Grand Prix circuit at Berne was 4.5 miles long, fast and had a bad record of racing accidents. Part of the course was cobbled and an invitation to slide in the rain. It was attractively located in a wooded area. On July 2nd and 3rd the annual weekend of speed took place with sportscar and Grand Prix car races as well as the motorcycle events.

The weekend started with 125cc and 250cc races. These were dominated by Italian machines and riders, with the exception of Fergus Anderson, third in the 250 race on a Guzzi. Next was the 350 race: Les, Bill Doran and Reg Armstrong rode factory 7Rs, Frith, Foster and Kenneth Bills rode works Velocettes and the familiar trio of Daniell, Bell and Lockett rode for Norton.

It was Bell who led away from the start, but not for long. Les stuck his head behind the flyscreen and caught up and passed Bell before the end of the first lap. Doran and Armstrong moved up ahead of Bell, while Freddie Frith was only eighth. Frith worked up to sixth on lap five, then took off! In one lap he passed Tommy Wood, Bell, Armstrong and Doran and started to catch Graham, which he did on lap twelve. The AJS group closed up and Doran nipped in front of Les for a moment, but Frith drew ahead to win by three seconds, Les recovered second place, less than a second ahead of Doran and Armstrong came third. Frith made fastest lap - and all three AJS riders finished.

There was a challenge from two factory Gileras, two factory Guzzis, and two twin cam Velocettes to

At Clady again, Les is flat on the tank on his way to win the 1949 Ulster. He was led by Pagani briefly on lap one, but took and kept the lead up to the finish. *FoTTofinders*

the AJS twins of Les and Ted Frend in the 500 race. The two Gilera fours followed Ted Frend and Les from the start, but Frend opened up his lead, while Bandirola on one of the Gilera fours departed with one of his not infrequent crashes, for which he was known in Italy as "il impetuoso Bandirola" and less grandly by British riders as "bouncing Bandi". This eliminated a useful group of competitors including Johnnie Lockett – none badly hurt – while Frend forged ahead followed by Les, Artesiani (Gilera) and Daniell. On lap 15 Frend ran out of road, fortunately missing all the trees, but having established fastest lap of the race at 90.60 mph. Les won by 22 seconds from Artesiani, Daniell, Pagani on a single cylinder Gilera and Frith.

At Assen, home of the Dutch TT, 100,000 spectators watched another hard-fought race in the 350 class. Once again Les was in front by the end of the first lap but the AJS machines were not running well. Frith was the tiger this time, moving into the lead on lap two, followed by Foster, Lockett, Doran and the rest. Rod Coleman made his Grand Prix debut but fell on lap five, while Les dropped further and further back. Doran also fell, like Coleman without injury and Frith and Foster took a breather from fighting for first place for a few laps, knowing they were closely matched. A last spurt and Frith took the race by nearly two seconds. Les' misfire had changed to

no fire at all, and Frend and Armstrong finished sixth and eighth.

In the 500 class Les and Doran rode the AJS twins. Twin cylinder Guzzis were ridden by Bob Foster and Lorenzetti, Gilera fours by Artesiani and Nello Pagani, Velocettes by Frith and Bills, and Nortons by the usual suspects. Once again Les led at the end of lap one, but this time after a furious dash after the speeding Gilera fours of Artesiani and Pagani. Les and the two Gileras pulled away from the field. It appeared that the Gilera riders were confident that they had the faster motorcycles and were sitting on Les' tail until they were ready to advance. Artesiani decided he might run out of fuel and made a quick pit stop, and both the Guzzis and Doran's AJS retired. In the lead on the last lap, Les knew that Pagani was close enough to pull by on the final long straight, which is exactly what he did, to win by over two seconds. Artesiani was back from the pits to finish third. Now it looked as if the Gileras were faster than the Porcupine, and the relegation of Pagani to Gilera singles had been lifted. Next weekend was to be the Belgian Grand Prix.

This event was held on the sweeping bends of the Spa-Francorchamps course in the Ardennes. Nine miles of excellent public roads were closed for the race, which vied with the Monza and Ulster courses

Close racing! Bill Doran tries to shake off Bertacchini (Guzzi) at Monza in the 1949 Italian Grand Prix. He succeeded, finishing third with the Guzzi 16 seconds behind. *Gianni Perrone*

for the title of "Europe's fastest road race." The same teams and riders who had raced in Holland reappeared, and the 350 race was again a close one. Foster took the lead until he touched a valve when he missed a gear, and Lockett, Bell, Frith and Graham streamed past him to swap the lead for a few laps. Ted Frend had a coming together with Foster which brought him but not Foster down, and Les retired with unspecified trouble. Foster recovered enough to move up to second place and the final order was Frith, Foster and Lockett, all inside 30 seconds.

In the 500 race Artesiani (Gilera) pulled ahead up the long uphill bend after the start, followed closely by the Nortons of Bell and Lockett and the Gilera of Pagani. Doran and Graham were next, with Lorenzetti (Guzzi twin,) Daniell and Fergus Anderson (Guzzi single,) all within striking distance. Les worked up to second place behind Artesiani before the end of the first lap and overtook him early in the third and Doran passed Pagani into fourth. Lorenzetti displaced Lockett in sixth place, and these six riders each led or came close to leading in a race-long battle. Les dropped to sixth place when he overshot a corner and was making up lost ground when a split tank forced him to retire.

Doran took the lead from Artesiani, but in the tenth lap Lorenzetti passed the Gilera, then Doran. This was one of the Guzzi twin's best races in 1949; like the AJS and Nortons, it seemed perfectly geared for Spa, while the Gileras had none of the superior speed they had in hand in Holland. Close racing between the leaders continued into the last lap and Artesiani and Lorenzetti approached the final hairpin at La Source together, Doran only a wheel behind. The

two Italians came into the bend too fast and went wide, letting Doran slip by on the inside and use all his revs to finish 0.2 seconds ahead of Artesiani and Lorenzetti. Bell's fourth place was as good as the works Nortons seemed capable of and Pagani was not pleased with his fifth place.

It had been a tremendous race for Doran, and a crucial win in the World Championship, as it left this contest open, with only two more races, the Ulster Grand Prix in August and the Italian Grand Prix early in September, left in the series. Artesiani, Pagani and Les led the Championship chase.

"The Ulster," was run on August 21st in untypically fine weather. There were some interesting changes in the teams, mainly additions: Gilera entered Pagani, Artesiani, Bandirola and Fusini, Moto Guzzi had Bob Foster and Bertacchini, Norton the usual trio, and AJS had Graham, Doran, Frend, Reg Armstrong and, in his old role of team manager and team member, Jock West. This team had three of the most forceful riders of the day, Les, Bill Doran and Ted Frend. Ted Frend and Armstrong were to ride 350cc 7Rs in the Junior race which was concurrent with the Senior GP. Compared to modern Grands Prix the race was a marathon of 247 miles, not quite as long as the Senior TT which was 264.5 miles, but long enough.

Off went the 250s, then the 350s, then lastly the 500s, round the 16.5 mile course. Both Les in the 500 and Frith in the 350 class broke the lap records from the standing start and led after their first laps. Bandirola and Pagani wound up their Gileras on the Clady straight to follow 7 seconds behind Les, with Artie Bell and Bob Foster in pursuit. Pagani almost

Reg Armstrong, Ted Frend and Les Graham parade to the start of the Italian grand Prix at Monza. Les was knocked off his machine while leading by a heroic passing manoeuvre by Bandirola, which also brought Bandirola down. *Gianni Perrone*

kept up with Les on the following laps. Bob Foster did his usual routine of hovering around sixth place for a few laps then lapping faster than anyone else to catch up with the leader. After five laps the order was Les, Foster, Pagani, then a cluster of riders, Bell, Doran, Artesiani and Lockett, all within one second, but 90 seconds behind Graham. Bandirola retired with ignition trouble, Foster ran out of fuel on lap 8.

At lap 10 of the 15 to be covered Les led by 1 minute 28 seconds from Artesiani and Bell and Pagani. Some of the fastest riders were timed over a quarter mile of the Clady straight: Pagani was fastest at 120.4 mph, while Les was timed at 119mph. Les, leading by one and a half minutes, eased off for the last four laps. Artesiani stopped with a carburettor problem on the last lap so the finishing order was Graham, Bell, Pagani, Doran and Jock West. All three AJS team riders finished, and in high positions. The result was a credit to Matt Wright as well as the riders. Most important, Les now held a lead over Pagani in the World Championship which could not be negated even if Les did not finish in the final Grand Prix and Pagani won.

Freddie Frith won the 350 Ulster Grand Prix, and having won all the other four qualifying races, became 350cc World's Champion, winning the

Manufacturers' Championship in the class for Velocette.

There was no 350cc class in the Italian Grand Prix des Nations at Monza on September 4th; this was an engine size regarded as superfluous in Italy as Italian 250cc machines were light, fast and popular, both for racing and road use.

Monza in 1949 was a four mile course in a park near Milan, which had been originally constructed in 1922 and rebuilt several times since. It had three slowish corners and several searingly fast bends which needed courage and correct gearing to negotiate really quickly. Norton, their machines lacking the pace of all the other factory racers, made no entries, AJS entered Les, Doran, and Armstrong on the twin cylinder 500s, Guzzi had Bertacchini, Leoni and Geminiani, and Gilera entered Pagani, Bandirola and Artesiani.

Artesiani led from the start followed by Pagani, Graham and Bandirola. On lap two Les gritted his teeth and passed the leading Gileras on one of the fast bends and began to draw away. On lap 5 Pagani managed to catch him, but Les repassed and headed a tight group of himself and the three Gileras. At this stage Bandirola decided to take the lead for Italy, whatever it took, and swept past Les on the

Les crouches low to keep his lead over Les Archer at Eppynt, "The Welsh TT." The narrow, bumpy circuit stretches away behind him as he keeps a finger on the clutch ready for any slides on the roughage.

entrance to one of the slow corners, failing to make the appropriate reduction in speed. He fell on the bend, his machine spinning in front of Les, who was thrown off his machine and although unhurt, found his AJS too badly damaged to continue. Bandirola broke his collar bone and retired.

The final winner at Monza was Pagani, followed by Artesiani, Bill Doran, the Guzzis of Leoni and Bertacchini, with Reg Armstrong taking fifth place on his Porcupine. The results of the World's Championship were unaffected by this result, but some Italians were unhappy that Les won his Championship by a single point from Pagani, a point earned by his fastest lap in the Swiss Grand Prix.

The fact that Les was skittled in the last race by a Gilera team rider while in the lead was forgotten.

Aside from the TT, the AJS twin had a good record of reliability in Grand Prix races in 1949. Compared to today's Moto Grand Prix machines, the factory racers of 1949 had a poor survival rate; one could expect one factory racer in five to break down while racing, partly because of the rough or bumpy surfaces of race tracks, partly because of design or metallurgic defects. Vibration was often accepted as unavoidable although it was a prime cause of engine or frame failure, and finances often excluded even a minor redesign when faults recurred. 1949 was the

best year of racing for the AJS twin and AJS made the most of it in advertising.

There were several minor races that Les took part in during the second half of the year. One of them was at Comminges, south of Toulouse and almost in the Pyrenees, on August 17th. It must have been another busman's holiday for Les, as it was a long way to haul a Porcupine and a 7R. Les found himself neck and neck with Tommy Wood and Georges Monneret in the 350cc race, swapping places and slipstreaming while M.D.Whitworth held the lead on his own Velocette. Les managed to squeeze ahead of his little group and came second, probably surprised to find such speed among the "Continental Circus." In the 500cc race Les had much more speed than his competitors and won from Whitworth on a Triumph and Fergus Anderson on the usual Moto Guzzi.

On September 24 Les revisited Shelsey Walsh, the 1000 yard hillclimb near Worcester. As before, the British Motor Cycle Racing Club challenged the British Racing Drivers Club (cars) and were represented by Les Graham, Freddie Frith, Triumph, and George Brown with a 1000cc Vincent - HRD. Sixteen motorcyclists took part, and special mention was made in the "Bemsee" journal of two newcomers who made fast times and showed promise of future distinction. They were Cecil Sandford (350 Velocette) and "Pip" Harris (596 Norton sidecar.)

Les ready to go at the September 24th hill climb at Shelsey Walsh. He broke the 350cc record on this 7R and the 500cc record on his Matchless, now fitted with rear springing.

"Les Graham had an AJS and the 500cc Matchless – this year fitted with rear springing. In practice the AJS was superior with good acceleration and seeming to handle more easily in the bend. The sheet of flame from its megaphone at the start caused the chock man considerable anxiety for his eyebrows. Both machines made records in their classes, the Matchless beating last year's figure by 1.26 seconds." Thus wrote the "Bemsee" journal. Les set new records for 350 and 500 machines, but the most impressive performance was that of George Brown, riding at Shelsey for the first time on an Vincent-HRD he had tuned himself and which was known as "Gunga Din". "Bemsee" journal reported; "George Brown did not do too well on his 500cc Vincent but his first run on "Gunga Din" was simply amazing. Little wheelspin, no lifting of the front wheel.... the way his helmet vanished into Kennel bend and was momentarily spotted was terrific – the great power allowed the least hesitation through the Esses." A smooth and masterly ascent, and a new absolute record for the hill, 22/100ths less than J.G.Fry's record time on his Freikaiserwagen. The cars won the two wheels versus four wheels match by 1.3 seconds from the motorcycles, based

on totalled times.

The BMCRC also organised the last major national event of the year – the Silverstone Autumn finale to the season, on October 8th. With the Norton team absent in France breaking long distance records at Montlehery track and no entries from Frith and Foster, the factory entries from AJS seemed certain to sweep the board. So they did in the 500cc race, the "Brooklands" race. Les Graham, Ted Frend and Bill Doran led from the start but they soon found Geoff Duke on his own Norton snapping at their heels. Geoff worked up to second place on his slower machine by fierce cornering, recalling Les Graham's prewar ability to get ahead of faster motorcycles on his OK Supreme at Donington and Cadwell. He finished a good fourth behind the AJS trio in a close race.

Silverstone confirmed the improvement in reliability of the AJS twins. There had been no breakdowns or frightening moments due to poor carburation. The outlook for 1950 was excellent, and it seemed that Nortons were the slowest machines in international racing.

Les kept his grip on the wet and poorly surfaced 1950 Swiss Grand Prix course at Geneva to win the race. The "dual carriageway" set up for the race can be seen with the straw bale dividers. *Gianni Perrone*

Nine

Changes and Controversy

1950 was to be another dramatic year in Grand Prix racing, but not for reasons that were welcome to the AJS team. There were incidents that denied good riders of results they deserved – perhaps more than usual – but the main problem for Les was that the AJS factory machines, 350cc and 500cc, were not as fast as their competitors.

"Windage", the odd term used by the motorcycling press for wind resistance, was recognised as a factor in speed by a few manufacturers, notably Moto Guzzi, and Norton and AJS added streamlined tails to their racers, while Moto Guzzi used a streamlined fuel tank that extended round and in front of the steering head. With their own wind tunnel for development of aerodynamics, only Guzzi realised that any amount of streamlining at the back of a vehicle was practically useless compared to reduction

and smoothing of the frontal profile. In spite of their good performance in 1949 AJS changed the position of the Porcupine's carburettors yet again, returning to long curved induction pipes and air intakes under the tank with a larger bore for the carburettors. The float chambers were attached to the frame rather than to the carburettors themselves to escape the effects of engine vibration. Maybe not the best idea in view of the bumps and vibration the frame itself suffered on the TT course.

Norton's new machines blew a gale of fresh air onto the racing scene: Rex McCandless' long-developed cradle frame with swinging arm rear springing was incorporated into a striking new design, which was thoroughly tested and approved pre-season at the Montlehéry track near Paris. In addition, the engine was revised by stiffening the crankshaft and flywheel

Norton *The World's Best Road-Holder*

"GEOFF DUKE – Winner of 1950 Senior T.T. at Record Speed 92·27 m.p.h.

The combination of Geoff Duke and the "featherbed" frame restored Norton to the top of international racing in 1950.

assembly to reduce internal flexion, and the cylinder head was extensively redesigned. Geoff Duke later acknowledged how lucky he was to have this machine to ride in his first year as a works rider.

Velocette fielded 350cc and 500cc machines again, with Bob Foster taking the place of Freddie Frith as team leader. After the departure of Remor, a relieved Luigi Gilera took over the design and development of the "four", whose cylinder-head was thoroughly revised and a new Marelli magneto was fitted. The new engine revved up to 9000rpm on test. The veteran Artesiani retired from the team to be replaced by 24 year old Umberto Masetti, and Piero Taruffi agreed to act as racing manager, in addition to his main employment as driver in the Ferrari Grand Prix team. Taruffi had raced the pre-war Gileras early in their development before the war and was also team manager in 1939 when Serafini won the European Championship.

The first British race meeting in which the AJS and Norton works riders met was at Blandford. The new Nortons finished first and second in the 500 race on their racing debut, Duke winning from Dickie Dale; in the 350 race Ted Frend won from Bob Foster and Geoff Duke. Les and Duke were both at Silverstone

but in separate 350 races over 8 laps which each won. There was no final but Les posted the faster race time, probably because he was chased all the way by Sid Barnett. Early in May Les took a 350 AJS to Eppynt to win both the 350 and the 500 races, shadowed once more in the latter by Sid Barnett on a 499cc Norton.

Then Les, Armstrong and Doran took the AJS van to Mettet. Les won the 350 race but was well beaten by Lorenzetti (Guzzi) in the 500 race. At Floreffe Doran won the 350 race from Les, who won the 500 race from Phil Heath and Reg Armstrong (who was riding a Triumph, which suggests that AJS sent only 350cc machines to these Belgian events.) By now, mid-May, preparations for the TT were under way and the modifications to the Porcupine needed to be completed and tested.

When Harold Daniell first saw the new works Norton he asked "Where's the step ladder?" referring to the higher saddle on the new machine. After riding it for a few laps he said it was like riding a featherbed, and "Featherbed" became the popular nickname for the Norton racer. In practice for the TT the weather was good and fast times were made by all AJS and

Airborn in the 1950 Ulster Grand Prix and carrying his 1949 winner's number !, Les struggled in vain to keep up with Geoff Duke. Both riders produced a string of 100mph-plus laps, the first on the post war Clady circuit. *FoTTofinders*

Norton team riders. Duke set the first 90mph lap speed since the war, but Doran crashed badly at the left-hander after Ballough bridge, breaking a leg. Although practice times can be deceptive, the Norton riders all looked more comfortable than Les and Ted Frend at similar speeds.

In beautiful weather, Nortons swept the board in both the 350cc race - Bell leading Duke and Daniell, with Les in fourth place after leading after the first lap, and in the 500cc race - Duke leading Bell and Lockett, with Les working up to fourth place. Les' average speed of 90.11 mph exceeded the fastest lap in 1949, but Duke's average of 92.27 mph set a new record, with a fastest ever lap of 93.3 mph. His riding was a sensation, comparable only to that of Freddie Frith in its consistency, fusion of several bends into one high speed swerve and smoothness of style. Joe Craig was a happy man; Jock West less so.

A Spanish Grand Prix took place near Barcelona on April 16. This did not count toward the World Championships and no British factory teams took the long journey to Montjuich Park. Tommy Wood won the 350cc race. Masetti led the 500cc race until his Gilera broke down on the last lap, giving the race to Nello Pagani.

The first Championship race after the TT was the Belgian Grand Prix. The first lap of the 350cc race saw Duke, Foster, Bell take the lead in turn, while Bill Lomas, riding for Velocette, caught up with the leaders and changed places with Duke and held third place. Foster seemed to have the fastest machine as well as his own great ability and led from half way to the finish. Duke edged past Lomas again to come third.

The 500cc race was a disaster for the British teams. First there was the infamous accident that eliminated Les and Artie Bell on the second lap. Geoff Duke, whom Les and Bell each had warned that Bandirola was prone to erratic speed changes, was closest behind the incident and described it in his autobiography "Pursuit of Perfection".

"On the climb (following Stavelot bend) Artie Bell steamed by and the order at the end of the first lap was: Bandirola, Bell, then me with Graham snapping at my heels.

"For the second time on the Masta straight, greater speed gave the Gileras command, with Les and Artie in their slipstream. Incredibly, after their dire warning to me at the start of the race, they both scooped up

At the right-hander at the end of the Clady straight Les lines up to accelerate after Duke. He finished second over a minute behind.
FoTTofinders

"Bandi" round the fast Stavelot Curve at the foot of the climb to Francorchamps' famous hairpin. With his four cylinder power, Bandirola promptly repassed them again on the next straight and all three dived together into the quick double left-hander near the top of the hill. Les was sitting on Bandirola's back wheel, with Artie a couple of yards behind and to Les' right. I was behind them – watching and wondering – positioned to Artie's left.

"Suddenly, Bandirola shut off his throttle. Les Graham had to brake violently and, locking the front wheel, his AJS twin went down, man and machine sliding off to the right. This left Artie Bell with no option. He had to try and get round the fallen Porcupine - but he had no chance. Graham was left lying in the road but his machine continued sliding along and was hit by Artie's Norton – who disappeared with both bikes in a cloud of dust beneath an elevated observation hut, which collapsed. Probably realising what had happened, Bandirola glanced back, and then pressed on."

Les escaped unhurt, but Bell had serious internal injuries and permanent damage to his right arm. That he recovered at all was largely due to his strong physique. Duke was horrified by what he saw and

set off after Bandirola in anger, convinced that the sudden stop was a deliberate ploy. Speeding after the Gilera, the second disaster struck Duke himself. Suddenly the rear tyre disintegrated, hurling a lump of tread at his backside. Lockett retired with the same problem, leaving the Gileras to take first, second, fourth and fifth places, with Ted Frend a good third. Masetti won, Pagani was second and Bandirola was fourth.

A week later at the Van Drenthe circuit in Holland, Dunlop provided new tyres for Norton and AJS with the assurance that they were absolutely sound. In the 350cc race this appeared to be true. Foster decided to skip his usual "watch and see" laps and went straight in front, where he stayed until the finish. Duke, Les and Bill Lomas had a fine battle for second place which ended for Les when his engine stopped on the next to last lap. The final order was Foster, Duke, Lomas and Lockett.

The 500cc race started well with Graham leading until Pagani and Bandirola passed him. Duke, Lockett and Masetti formed a second group until the fifth lap, when Duke had a spectacular crash, his Norton cartwheeling up the road when his rear tyre broke up. The tyres of Graham, Foster and the rest of

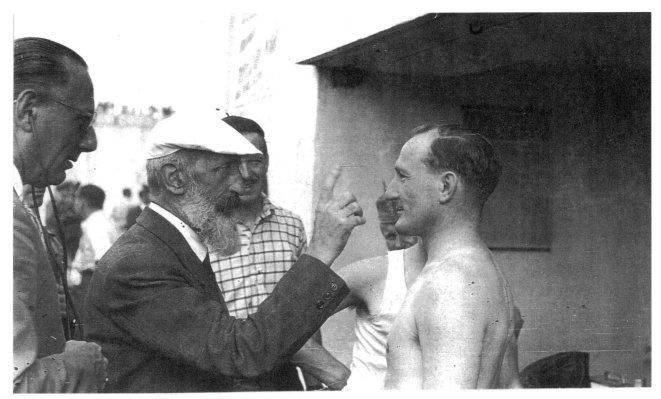

An outdoor eye test for Les before the 1950 Italian Grand Prix from Doctor Fenini. *Millanta*

the Norton team also gave up, presenting Gilera with another win. Masetti and Pagani headed the excellent Harry Hinton, Norton, at the finish, the Australian in turn heading Bandirola.

On to Geneva for the Swiss Grand Prix, on what must have been the worst circuit of any used for post war Grand Prix races. The course started near the station, then after a 90° bend, ran alongside Lake Geneva as far as a big roundabout opposite the impressive offices of the International Labour Organisation. The lakeside stretch was divided in two for all of its length by a single row of straw bales topped with sandbags, so that riders could come bombing back to the start and finish on the other side of the road, after negotiating a short wiggle after the ILO offices. Tramlines were present at several points.

 The circuit presented the kind of challenges that Les enjoyed. When it started raining just after the start of the 350 race he was in his element. He was first away, and in the right hand bend just after the start his AJS went into a huge slide from one side of the road to the other. Les managed to stay on board but seven riders fell, either on the greasy surface or in trying to avoid Les. Foster was one of them. They all picked themselves up and finished somewhere behind Graham. Foster got within 18 seconds of Les to take second place followed by Duke (now on Avon tyres,) Armstrong and Ted Frend.

The start of the 500cc race was also followed promptly by heavy rain. Masetti did well to keep his seat and lead after the first lap, but Les caught up quickly and the two circulated together until Les went wide on the narrow divided stretch and smacked into a straw bale. He pulled his machine out as the rain stopped and went after Masetti, catching and passing him to win the race. The final order was Graham, Masetti, Bandirola, Duke and Daniell. This was the first event in 1950 where Les was able to show his best form; it must have greatly improved his state of mind. The World's Championship leaders were Masetti and Geoff Duke, but the contest was still open.

The Ulster Grand Prix, on August 19, started in sunshine. Jock West, unable to shake off his love of racing, entered himself as well as Les Graham and Ted Frend in the 500cc race, with two new works entries, Cecil Sandford and the Australian, Eric McPherson, in the 350cc race. Pagani, Masetti and Bandirola represented Gilera, and Harry Hinton joined Duke, Lockett, Daniell and Dale in the Norton team. The absence of Artie Bell was strongly felt by his many admirers in the usual huge crowd. Cecil Sandford remembers that even in 1950, spectators on the Clady straight stood out on the road until riders appeared, stepping back as they came into sight.

Geoff Duke was the man of the day, breaking the

The Graham - Duke duel in the 350 Italian Grand Prix. Les minimises his wind-resistance, but it was not enough to overtake Duke. He came second. *Gianni Perrone*

lap record with a speed of 101.77 mph and leading on every lap except the sixth, when he refuelled and Les briefly led. Localised showers fell during lap two, giving many riders including Duke and West unpleasant moments when they slid at speed, and Bill Lomas and Ernie Lyons got too close and fetched each other off. Toward the end of the two and a half hour race the rain started to fall heavily, but Duke was far enough ahead to be able to ease off and still finish 45 seconds ahead of Graham. Both riders lapped at over 100mph on 8 laps, and exceeded 101mph on one lap. Third, fourth and fifth were Lockett, Dale and West, followed in turn by Masetti and Pagani. Bandirola fell off at Tully corner and was taken to hospital, but sent home later the same day.

Foster, of course, won the 350cc race followed by Armstrong and Hinton; Cecil Sandford finished fifth ahead of Daniell. Foster retired in the last Grand Prix of the 1950 World Championship in Italy. But he still was the Champion in the 350cc class, with 30 points against the second in the series, Geoff Duke.

The last Grand Prix was the Italian at Monza. The AJS team set out to Monza with most of the machines and two mechanics, one driving, in an ex-army Bedford truck and with two machines in an under - powered V8 Ford, which had an "upstairs" compartment with windows built across its width to accommodate the rest of the mechanics and riders. The route went over the spectacular Simplon Pass, but the high seats, roadside vertical drops and the truck's lack of power made for a journey that Cecil Sandford did not enjoy. Rod Coleman also experienced this truck, which he remembers for its poor reliability.

In Monza the sun shone over a day of fierce high-speed battles and a fierce controversy. Typically of Monza, the faster riders formed high-speed clusters once the 350cc race was under way. Hinton, Duke, Dale, Les and Lockett swapped places in the front group, Armstrong, Lomas and Sandford ran together a little way behind. Harry Hinton was the rider who impressed most in the 350cc race, shattering the lap record with a speed of 97.15mph, but in spite of lying feet stretched out rearwards to minimise "windage", he had to yield second place to Les who came second, himself exactly one second behind Duke. Monza's fast wide straights and bends always seemed to generate the closest racing of the season, with cars as well as motorcycles.

In the 500cc class Masetti started with a three point advantage over Duke. Monza suited the faster Gileras, so Geoff would need luck as well as skill to take the championship; Masetti would have to fail to finish at all for this to happen. Les was in third place in the Championship.

At the start of the 500cc race Bandirola made a

The 1950 Porcupine was not fast enough to keep up with the rejuvenated Nortons. At Monza Les could only manage 7th in the 500cc place. *Gianni Perrone*

lightning start, to be quickly passed by Duke and Masetti. The two contenders led Artesiani, (who appears to have "retired" from Gilera to MV Agusta) and Bandirola in a group of four, followed after five seconds by Lockett, Dale, Graham, Pagani and Milani (Gileras). Then Masetti and Duke broke away and the former set a new lap record of 105.44mph, pulling two seconds ahead of Duke. The pair led in turn, until after the half way mark, when Masetti started to lose speed. It seems that Masetti himself was losing strength; each lap was taking a little longer, and Duke was 50 seconds ahead as he approached the finish on the next to last lap. There seemed a real possibility that Masetti might not finish, in which case Duke would take the 500cc Championship.

To his and almost everyone else's surprise the chequered flag came out a lap early, signalling the end of the race. Joe Craig jumped out from the pits and frantically waved at Duke to carry on, but Duke had stopped, and by the time he saw Joe, Masetti had stopped too, and was being lifted from his machine. With the tact and diplomacy normal to the Motorcycle press in those days, no reports of the race suggested that the premature halt to the race was arranged to ensure that Masetti did not lose the last of his strength and retire before finishing that crucial 32nd lap. But the words used and later comments clearly showed that this was what everyone, including a crowd which

went absolutely silent, believed.

It is hard to believe that Taruffi, Gilera team manager and a man of apparent good sense and integrity, had a quiet word with the race organisers during lap 31, but it does seem that someone did. The board displaying the state of the race to the public clearly marked that there was one lap to go when the flag was displayed, but after an hour of argument, the representatives of the FIM confirmed that lap 31 was officially the last of the race, and that Masetti was the new World Champion.

And did it really matter in the longer term? Masetti rode superbly throughout 1950 and won just one more Championship in 1952. Geoff Duke went on to win a total of six Championships before retiring. Les, who finished seventh in the Italian grand Prix and third in the 500cc class of the World Championship, probably found the whole thing funny. He had realised that the nature of AJS management would make it impossible for the racing department to develop the 7R and Porcupine machines up to world-beaters, and was ready to accept an offer he had received to join MV Agusta to develop as well as ride their racing motorcycles. Before the end of year, he had signed the generous contract he had discussed with Domenico Agusta – "the Count", gentleman managing director of the company.

The AJS team competed at Mettet in 1950. Les won the 350cc race from Reg Armstrong and Geoff Duke on this 7R.

The 500cc race was won by Enrico Lorenzetti, Guzzi, by three seconds from Les, seen here leading Bill Doran past the usual crowds of spectators.

The MV Agusta team, not including Les, at Monza for pre-season testing in 1951. Bandirola looks full of confidence, second from left, and to his left is Artesiani, former Gilera rider. The MV looks massive, if handsome.

Ten

The Italian Job

Les Graham's contract of employment with MV was regarded by some of the more jingoistic motorcycle enthusiasts as a compact with the devil. Those who followed racing closely and knew of Ernie Lyons, Freddie Frith, Bob Foster, Fergus Anderson and many others who rode for Italian companies wished Les good luck - certainly better than in 1950.

In fact he was now working not so much for a company as for a family - a large family with all the energy and tensions that large families can generate. Four brothers ran the company, led by Domenico Agusta, the oldest. Their father, Count Giovanni, had

founded an aircraft company seven years before the first world war, in which he was a fighter pilot, which built a large three-engined aircraft, as well as parts, and did contract engineering for the industry. When Giovanni Agusta died at 48 in 1927, Domenico took over and went on producing parts for aircraft into the second world war. His passion was for motorcycles and during the war he drew up and made a prototype 98cc two-stroke, from which a production model was manufactured in 1946. Confusingly, it was called the "Vespa".

Interest in motorcycles returned with a bang in Italy

Les on the MV before going out for practice for the 1951 TT. He worked up to fifth place at the end of lap 2 but then retired with valve trouble.

in 1946, and sport and sales were surprisingly strong. The company was renamed "Meccanica Verghera" in 1945, Verghera being the location of the factory in northern Italy. A series of sporty-looking two strokes sold well, and a racing version of these was quite successful until the Mondial and Morini OHC 125s dominated this class. In 1949 Piero Remor joined MV straight from Gilera, with a brief to produce a four cylinder racing machine and an overhead camshaft 125 based on a quarter of the "four." Both were destined for a works racing team and for sale to private owners. The engine and frame of the four looked as if they were taken straight from the 1949 Gilera; a one-piece cylinder head, two carburettors, pressed steel forks with central spring and limited travel friction-damped rear springing. The gearbox was all new. Final drive was by shaft, necessitating a complex gearbox with the necessary bevel gears to deliver motive power at right – angles to the crankshaft. Power loss, torque reaction from the shaft and universals, and difficulty in changing gear ratios for different circuits were features of this transmission. Strangely, there were two foot-change pedals, one for up and one for down, on opposite sides of the machine. This must have kept the feet busy when braking hard for slow corners.

MV entered the bike in several Grands Prix in 1950, ridden by Artesiani and Leoni, and on one occasion by Reg Armstrong. Artesiani finished well in the Belgian and Italian Grands Prix, but for the most part the season was one of gear selection problems and failure to start in races for which they had been entered. Domenico had high hopes that Les would help solve these problems, and the two developed a firm friendship and respect for one another. How different from the directors of AJS and Norton!

But there was no magic to improve things overnight. For 1951 the number of races counting toward the World's Championship was increased to eight, with the addition of the Spanish, and German Grands Prix. Les' record for the series was a complete wipe-out: Spanish GP, retired: Swiss GP, retired while in second place; Senior TT, retired from fifth place on lap three; Dutch TT, retired; Italian GP, retired; French, German and Ulster GPs, did not start. A third place on one of MV's 125cc machines in Holland, a second in the 350cc race in Spain, and a win in the same class in the Swiss Grand Prix on a private Velocette were the only glimmers in this dismal record.

There had been some light relief early in the year

Picture of a brave man. Les at high speed on Bray Hill, his front wheel clear of the ground. The awkward rear suspension on the drive side did not help Les on the Mountain course.

when Les was joined by his family, including his wife's sister, Barbara, for the races at Mettet and Floreffe, as well as two races in Italy . Barbara was staggered at the quality and availability of food in Belgium, in contrast to the fairly severe rationing which was still in force in Great Britain. The "continental circus" were there in force, and Geoff Duke was also there to experience the jolly atmosphere for the first time. At Mettet it snowed before the 350cc race, but the organisers had no hesitation in starting the race. Cecil Sandford looked at Les, who seemed unconcerned and decided to follow in his tracks. There can have been no surface that Les had not experienced in his seventeen years of racing, and by the time the snow had melted, he was well ahead of the field on his Velocette. Then Bill Doran on a works AJS caught and passed him, and Les finished second, just ahead of Duke. At Floreffe Cecil Sandford won the 350c race by a whisker from Reg Armstrong's works AJS.

The next race was the Swiss Grand Prix at Berne,

where it rained hard. Helped by magneto failures which eliminated the Norton team, Les worked up to second place by the fourth lap, only to crash on the next lap, when he slid off at 120mph, he and the MV continuing side-by-side down the wet road, damaging the MV and skinning Les' ankle through his boot. Fergus Anderson rode an excellent race on the Guzzi vee-twin, winning by nearly two minutes from Armstrong's Porcupine. Les won the 350cc race from Sandford, both on works Velocettes.

The Swiss Grand prix actually overlapped the beginning of TT practice, and there was no time for the usual transport of men and machines by road and ferry to the Isle of Man, so an aircraft was chartered to take most of the British riders and bikes to Ronaldsway airfield. Joe Craig and the Norton riders were already unhappy about the Norton magneto failures in the races when they arrived at Berne airport, and were even less happy when they saw their aircraft. It was a DC3 Dakota freighter, with no

Landing neatly on both wheels at Ballough, Les looks ahead to the Sulby straight, where the MV's terrific yowl will please the spectators.

fixed passenger seats and precious little space for the intended load.

Thirteen men and thirteen machines were intended to go. One rider withdrew when he added up the number of passengers. The remainder decided to put the benches provided along the sides of the Dakota, and the bikes across the middle. Cecil Sandford, who thoroughly enjoyed the experience, and Geoff Duke, described the flight. The load was the absolute maximum for the DC3, and the pilot showed concern for the length of the runway. He borrowed a jeep to check it, then started his take-off run hard by the perimeter wall of the airfield. Duke felt the Dakota would never leave the soggy grass of the airfield, but it did, clearing the far perimeter fence by a few feet.

Les and Tommy Wood, both ex-RAF pilots, took it on themselves to give a running commentary on the proceedings, which made nobody feel any better, least of all Joe Craig, who hated flying anyway. A stop at

Brussels was needed as the pilot had pumped some fuel out at Berne to get within the maximum flying weight, then it was on to the Island. Geoff Duke, having a turn in the co-pilot's seat, saw London brilliantly lit up for the Festival of Britain, and his flight was not spoiled by the antics of Tommy and Les.

The Dakota approached Ronaldsway in thick cloud, toward midnight. One version of the story says that Tommy and Les peered intently out of the window, then found their luggage and took out their crash helmets and put them on. The pilot, with no navigator or co-pilot, made a perfect landing. A silent and rigid Joe Craig was helped from his seat and the journey to Douglas was completed by road.

In the Junior TT Les was tenth, behind Rod Coleman and Ray Amm, who were making their TT debuts before going on to make their mark as works riders and TT winners. In the Senior, Les had the ridiculous starting number of 90. He would not have to overtake

Les got to know most of the Italian car racing drivers, and was interested in the possibility of racing cars himself in the future. This is one of the last 158/159 supercharged Alfa Romeos built before Alfa Romeo gave up Grand Prix racing.

88 riders to win, but he would have to pass an awful lot of them! Perhaps this was the ACU's punishment for "going foreign". The ACU was very slow to recognise how unhelpful their numbering could be; in 1950 almost every works rider had more than 50 riders in front of them at the start; even works riders take risks when passing on the Isle of Man.

The best that Les could achieve for the rest of the season was seventh place in the 350cc class of the Italian Grand Prix. The 500cc MV was plagued by gearbox and other problems, but Les assured Domenico Agusta that the machine was capable of winning, and he renewed his contract with MV for 1952. He had clear ideas of what was necessary to make a first class racer of the four, and Domenico was prepared to put his recommendations into effect. Remor was still development engineer at MV, but the changes that transformed the machine for the 1952 season almost all originated with Les.

Like Gilera in the same year, MV fitted one carburettor to each cylinder in place of one carb feeding two cylinders. Otherwise the engine was hardly altered. The frame was completely revised, to a lighter, fully tubular design with swinging arm rear suspension, modelled on the Norton featherbed. The disastrous shaft drive transmission was thrown out, having proved itself unsuitable for racing, and was replaced with a five speed box (with only one gear-change pedal) and chain drive. Les liked suspension with more travel than most racing bikes provided, and he was attracted to the special "leading link" fork designed and made by Ernie Earles. One of these forks was fitted to a 500cc BSA raced successfully by Charlie Salt in 1951, and Les visited the Earles

establishment to arrange for one to be made for the MV.

One interesting aspect of joining MV Agusta was meeting the men who raced for the firm, mostly in the 125cc class. A particularly interesting team-mate was Carlo Bandirola, whose do-or-die tactics had twice fetched Les off his AJS in major races; Monza in 1949 and Belgium in 1950. Bandirola was anxious to explain how these crashes happened, and Les accepted that they were the results of bad judgement and too much adrenaline. Bandirola and Les communicated in sign language and Italian in equal measures, and became good friends. "A smashing fella" was the opinion of Cecil Sandford, and of Les' sister in law, Barbara, later a frequent visitor to "Casa Gram", as the Graham house was locally called.

In the winter of 1951-1952 Les must have felt that his skill and determination were at last getting serious recognition. He was admired internationally as a rider of the highest class, in spite of bad luck; he had a free hand in the development of a very fast motorcycle, and he had the support and confidence of his family and his employer. Looking ahead, a new possibility was presented by invitations to test-drive the sports-racing cars of Jaguar and Aston Martin, both of whom were running full-time teams in the international Sports Car Championship. Les drove an Aston Martin and a Jaguar that winter on separate occasions, and John Wyer of Aston Martin and F. R. W. "Lofty" England of Jaguar wrote to say that they were impressed. As Les was happy at MV at the time, no commitment was made except to ask Les to consider driving as reserve driver if either of the teams found themselves short of a team member. As a friend of Raymond Mays and his sons, the possibility of Les driving a BRM was also mentioned but came to nothing.

Les had always been very loyal to AJS as a racing team member, probably through friendship with Jock West. He made no criticism of the company or its machines when he left to join MV. He was an optimist in racing matters, and indeed most other matters as well. One of the few things he would not tolerate was officious race organisers who made life difficult for competitors, but otherwise he accepted misfortunes that would turn another man's hair grey as his own fault, or just part of life's rich pattern. The AJS works riders who were still plagued by continuing magneto faults in 1951 and 1952 were not so upbeat about their experiences.

Now all this was behind him. Les' loyalty was now to MV, where he had authority and the respect due to the man who would make the company a leader in motorcycle racing.

Bill Doran was an excellent, tough rider and he, Les and Ted Frend made a formidable AJS team before Les left for MV. Here at Bray Hill, he was second in the 1951 Senior TT.

The 1951 MV out in the wide open spaces of Silverstone at the end of the season. Once again, Les retired with gearbox troubles.

Cecil Sandford and Les at the frame-building works of Ernie Earles, discussing the forks that Les thought would improve the MV's roadholding. The aircraft type bolts holding the telescopics in the forks are inset and seem unlikely to come undone.

The MV Agusta four transformed under Les' instructions early in the 1952 Senior TT. Most of the changes from 1951 are visible, including the Earles front fork, the lighter tubular frame with one swinging rear suspension arm, the separate carburettors for each cylinder and the lower, compact build of the machine. *FoTTofinders*

Efforts Rewarded

At meetings of the FIM late in 1951, the motorcycle manufacturers who competed in the World's Championship argued for a return to six qualifying events in 1952 instead of the eight of 1951. Too much time was spent travelling instead of competing in national events, which had as much publicity value in the home country as international races, while some events, notably the Swiss Grand Prix and the Isle of Man TT were so close in time that machine preparation was said to suffer. This was a plus rather than a minus for teams that normally gave the TT a miss, but Italian participation in the TT became stronger from 1951, and anyway, the FIM did not usually listen very hard to manufacturers' complaints. Eight events it was, again, in 1952.

Very sensibly, MV decided to field a team of only two to begin with, of Les and his new-found friend Carlo Bandirola. Neither had any success in the early minor international races, Codogno or Mettet. At Mettet Les took an early lead, but Rod Coleman caught up, and he recalls trying to pass and being showered by stones from the verges of the road as Les swung from side to side of the track. Rod did not like this, not surprisingly, and after the race (which he won) he found Les and told him so. According to Rod, Les did not appreciate being told how to ride and answered along the lines of "Sonny, when you have ridden as long as I have.....". This did not help matters as Rod was no green rooky, but as both were intelligent riders, they settled their differences and Les said he would rather be told than learn later of someone's annoyance with him..

Les planned to ride a works-supplied 250cc Velocette in 1952 and is here at the Velocette factory with it. Behind him are Bertie Goodman, (striped tie,) racing and development manager and Edna Graham. Les' fourth place in the Lightweight TT was Velocette's best TT result in the last year of their racing department.

Rod Coleman was one of the overseas riders who were rapidly matching the best of the Europeans in skill, and exceeding some of them in determination. There were also European newcomers who impressed; Dave Bennett, who earned a place in the Norton team, D. K. Farrant, who was to race for AJS, and the German, Werner Haas, who seemed to appear from nowhere to start winning Grand Prix races. In Italy Tarquino Provini and Emilio Mendogni joined the many gifted riders contending in national as well as international championships.

As mentioned earlier, Les believed in helping new riders to make progress, and this included more experienced riders riding for the first time on a circuit familiar to Les, but not to them. The "tuck in behind me" signal was often given to such riders during practice, Les then leading through the circuit on what he considered the best racing line at a speed they could keep up with.

Several interesting machines made a first appearance in the 1952 Swiss Grand Prix. The most radical was an ultra-light 350cc three cylinder DKW two-stroke. This little machine reintroduced the deafening DKW scream of prewar days, but it took another three years before it featured in Grand Prix results. There were also a lean 350cc single and a chunky 500cc Horex twin which finished well in their first major race, ridden by Schnell and Schon. Benelli entered two of the new version of their 1939 TT-winning single; one was offered to Les and in spite of losing top gear on this fast circuit, he finished third behind two Guzzis. Some attention had been paid to streamlining by several teams including Gilera and MV; this was mostly in the form of rounded fuel tanks that surrounded the steering head, but Guzzi remained the only competitor to use streamlining based on wind tunnel trials. The 1952 Gilera developed up to 58bhp at 10,000rpm and one can assume that the new MV was close in power output. Norton engines had

At Quarter Bridge in the later stages of the 1952 TT the flattened exhausts of the MV show how hard Les was riding.

received their usual winter development, mainly to the frame and carburation, but there was no news of a new multi-cylinder engine. The Norton singles were still remarkably fast.

In the fifties the "technical" press seemed very interested in competing machines' horsepower, but only occasionally speculated on the maximum speeds these horsepowers achieved. A rare timed kilometre taken from Cromie McCandless on a Gilera in the 1952 Ulster showed a speed of 127. 2mph on the bumpy Clady straight. On a smoother road the maximum would have been higher - perhaps 135 to 140mph, which was likely to be equalled by the MV.

The 500cc MV was a vastly improved motorcycle. In the 500cc Swiss Grand Prix Les set off in hot pursuit of Geoff Duke in the main event. He was forced to retire with tyre trouble after five laps, either because the rear Dunlop fouled the mudguard or the tyre broke up. Bandirola finished a good third at an average speed above the previous lap record. On the next to last lap Norton's new team member, Dave Bennet, was running third close behind two of the works AJS, trying to get the better of Doran and Jack Brett, two experienced campaigners. He lost control on the fast twists that had seen three fatal crashes since 1947 and was killed.

In June came Les' chance to win a TT after 14 attempts. In six of these he retired through mechanical breakages, only one of which could be blamed on his vigorous style. Les counted the Isle of Man and the Swiss circuit of Berne as his favourite road races. This time he knew he had a machine as fast as any in the Senior TT, and he probably reckoned Geoff Duke to be the only rider as fast as himself. In the event Geoff Duke was faster than Les on each of the first four laps, then Geoff's clutch bearings gave up. This put Les in the lead, only twelve seconds ahead of Reg Armstrong, who was riding at his very best. Fast though Les was lapping, averaging 93.66 on his third lap, oil on the change pedal caused a missed change and enough engine damage to lose about 800rpm, enough to lose the edge on the Norton on acceleration.

On the sixth lap Les and Reg raced side by side along the Sulby straight, Les having started 20 seconds after Reg. Beside the loss of revs, the MV's rear tyre had almost no tread left and as Les kept with Reg round Sulby Bridge and led him into Ramsey he was calculating the risks of going all out on a bald-tyred, slightly underpowered machine, as against a safe second place. He chose the safer option, probably thinking of Edna waiting at the finishing line and two little boys at home, and he watched Armstrong draw away, out of sight, to finish 26 seconds ahead of

At Union Mills the MV is airborn while Les appears in control and very determined.

him - a worthy winner. The primary chain on Reg's Norton broke at the very moment that he crossed the line, the kind of luck that rarely came Les' way!

MV had two 125cc machines on the Island and Les had his 250cc Velocette. Cecil Sandford practiced on the MV at a modest speed. The 125cc and 250cc races were run at the same time, the 250s starting before the 125s, and Les kept his options open until two days before these events. It is surprising that the organisers allowed this flexibility, considering their traditional refusal of late entries. Les opted for the Velocette - a wrong choice perhaps, as Cecil Sandford made nonsense of his low practice speeds and led Ubbiali and two other works Mondials to win at 75.5 mph, faster than most of the 250 finishers. Another MV came fifth, ridden by A. A. Copeta on his first visit to the TT.

Cecil Sandford was recognised by Les as a very promising rider, and the two got on well. Les passed on his experience of circuits and of coping with bad racing conditions. In those days racing went on whatever the weather and however bad the track conditions. There was no suggestion of stopping racing for melted tar or greasy roads, and the TT was no better than any other race at this time. Another younger rider "adopted" by Les was Derek Farrant, winner of the 1952 500cc Manx

Grand Prix and later a successful member of the AJS works team.

The spectators were treated to a classic demonstration of riding to team orders in the 250cc TT. There were five works Guzzi riders, but it was said that Guzzi had nominated Fergus Anderson to be winner of the race, and he led after the first lap. Then Bruno Ruffo, a gifted and daring rider, decided to hurry up, break the lap record and built up a lead of 20 seconds at the start of the fourth and last lap. Strangely, he took an extra four minutes to cruise round the last lap, watching four team-mates and Les Graham go by. This was the approved method of obeying team orders while giving maximum offence to the winner and the man who gave the order. In the same situation in the 1968 125cc TT, Bill Ivy added the refinement of actually stopping on the last lap at Creg-ny-Baa and asking the spectators who was winning, after he was told to let Phil Read win the race.

In 1952 Les was a good fourth in the 250 TT against faster Guzzis. In Holland he could only manage seventh place in the 500cc race and retired in the 250 event. Belgium provided a sixth in the 250 race but he did not finish on the 500 MV. Meanwhile Sandford won two of the three World's Championship races in the 125cc class for MV and came third in the third, putting himself well ahead in points.

At the finish of the 1952 TT Les congratulates Reg Armstrong on his Senior TT victory. Geoff Duke, to Reg's right, had one of his rare TT retirements. Behind him to his right is Rex McCandless and behind Edna Graham is Gilbert Smith, Managing Director of Norton.

Next came the German Grand Prix, on a very poor surface at Solitude. Huge crowds estimated at 400,000 attended, many of them camping the night before the race, and straw bales intended to protect spectators found their way into many tents for bedding. The bales would have made little difference to the spectators sitting three feet from the action round most of the track; miraculously none of the many crashes took riders into the crowd. Among those who crashed were Ray Amm, Rod Coleman, Masetti., Milani (Gilera solo), Milani (Gilera sidecar), Ruffo and Lorenzetti, (who made contact during a fierce duel,) Brett, Lomas, Wunsche, and Ernie Ring. Les, perhaps profiting again from his familiarity with loose surfaces, made fastest lap of the day and finished fourth in the 500cc race. The organisers would not wait for him to bring his Velocette round to the start of the 250cc race after his 125cc MV blew up on the far side of the course, and started without him, the kind of thing Les did not accept gracefully.

German riders and machines delighted spectators in the 125 and 250cc races; Werner Haas beat the Italians in the 125 race, and a Guzzi wipe-out allowed Felgenheier (DKW), to win and Gablenz

(Horex) to take third place in the 250 race. This was to be the prelude of a brief golden age for German manufacturers, particularly NSU, who threw themselves into international competition with varying success. NSU were ahead of any other firm in innovation and development, but sales did not keep pace with their expenditure on racing and record-breaking, a familiar story.

As team manager as well as leading rider in the MV team, Les Graham had reason for satisfaction with the season's achievements so far, in spite of not winning the TT. He personally had finished in a respectable place in four out of five 500cc Grands Prix, something that had never happened at AJS; his choice of Cecil Sandford to ride the MV 125cc machines had brought wins and a lead in the 125cc World's Championship, which must have been a welcome surprise, given the record of the Mondial racers in that class and the brilliance of Ubbiali as a rider. Three races remained.

Les wanted to make sure that Cecil won the 125cc Championship and asked Bill Lomas to join the MV team for the Ulster Grand Prix, both as back up for

Fergus Anderson was a fine rider and had a long career including riding for the German NSU factory in the 1930s. He stayed with Moto Guzzi from the late 1940s until 1955, winning the 1953 350cc World's Championship for them, and is here, sitting, with his team-mate and friend Enrico Lorenzetti.

Sandford and to strengthen the 500cc team, (although Bandirola was less "impetuoso" than he had once been.) Lomas jumped at the offer, and joined the Graham family at a hotel convenient for the Boreham airfield circuit. Edna Graham and the boys, Stuart and Christopher were also there. Although only 7 and 10, both boys had ridden a racing machine, sitting in front of Les. Bill rode the MV Les had for the race at Boreham – a hybrid shaft-drive machine with Earles Forks – before the race and found it smooth, powerful and responsive. He accepted Les' offer and went to Belfast with Cecil Sandford and Les for "the Ulster".

Bill had his first experience of a racing 125 in Ulster, where Sandford taught him to use maximum revs almost all the time, using the five gears to get the speed appropriate for the situation on the road. They were able to take the Clady straight and its bumps flat out without any speed wobble on landing, and the high cornering speed came as a surprise, as it does to anyone watching modern 125s swoop round bends.

Bill also liked the 500cc MV "four", until he hit one of the Clady bumps at a speed he put at "nearly

145mph." The MV flew in the air, which Bill was prepared for, but went into a horrible wobble or tank-slapper on landing, which lasted 100 frightening yards. Les said that he had no trouble and that Bill should not grip the handlebars so tightly. This did not work for Bill, who found the bumps terrifying, but he clearly resolved the problem himself as he finished third in the Ulster Grand Prix. He still disliked the Earles forks on corners, as he believed that the weight of the fork behind the line from steering head to front spindle was enough to give heavy steering.

Les broke the lap record for the Clady course at 105.94mph, which still stands, as the course was changed next year. He retired while leading when either rear tyre failure or the rear mudguard caused the tread to fly off. Les was not going to blame Dunlop, who had given him so much help since the war. Cecil Sandford won the 125cc race and the World's Championship ahead of two more MVs. Ubbiali fell off on a corner that Lomas discovered could be taken faster by mounting the pavement where the curb was low. Ubialli tried the same maneouvre but did not spot the point where the curb had been worn away so the resulting bump unseated him.

Umberto Masetti, World's Champion on Gileras in 1952. He beat Les Graham by only three points for the Championship. He is seen before and during the 1952 German Grand Prix.

Rod Coleman was by far the most successful AJS rider in 1952 in both 350cc and 500cc classes. In 1954 he won the Junior TT. Here he is after coming third in the 1952 Junior on the three valve AJS. Behind his helmet is Matt Wright, in leathers is Bill Lomas, who was fourth.

Two Championship races remained, the Italian Grand Prix des Nations, and the Spanish Grand Prix at Barcelona. As usual the Italian factories each entered a fleet of machines at Monza in the hope of wearing out the opposition. Les entered himself as well as Bill Lomas and Cecil Sandford in the 125cc race, and tried each of the five machines available to ensure that he got the best or one of the best. In a very close race, Les scrambled into the lead by the start of the last lap. Ubbiali scrambled past him and finally, within sight of the finish, a little known rider, Emilio Mendogni, steamed past them both and won. All three finished inside a half-second as if it were a 100 meter dash. Morini only entered two machines, which finished first and fourth.

MV prepared five machines for the 500cc race. Two of them had telescopic forks, at the request of Bandirola and Gianni, but Lomas was obliged to start with the Earles forks, which were becoming something of an obsession with him.

It seemed that everyone wished Les a win in the race. His hard work and bad luck had been followed by the Monza crowd, and they cheered him when he came by in the lead at the end of the first lap. There he stayed until the finish, pulling away to finish over a

mile ahead of a battle for second between Bandirola, Pagani and Masetti. The crowd was delighted, for to them he was an Italian by adoption; most of the Agusta family and Les' wife Edna were at the finish to congratulate him at the high point of his and MV's motorcycling career.

There was a possibility that Les might win the 500cc World's Championship if he won the Spanish Grand Prix at Barcelona and Masetti and Armstrong did not finish. It did not happen, but the end of the season was turning out too well for MV for any disappointment when they both finished the race.. They were behind Les, who won on the extremely twisty and slow Montjuich circuit at 59.54mph. He also finished second in the 125cc race, which was won by Mendogni on a Morini. Mendogni's average speed for the race was 58.29 mph showing how fast the little bikes could corner.

So ended the most successful and stimulating year of Les' career. He had not won the TT, nor the World's Championship, but the stirring finish to the 1952 season was deeply satisfying and brought joy to MV and the racing enthusiasts of Italy and Great Britain.

The Swiss Grand Prix, Berne, 1952. Les was offered one of the latest factory Benellis for the 250cc class of this race, and is seen on the grid, (No.22) with a second Benelli on his left. He chased Fergus Anderson (Guzzi) who was leading in the first few laps, then lost fifth gear and finished a good third.

Ken Kavanagh takes fast bend in the 1952 German Grand Prix at Solitude. He was second to Reg Armstrong in the 350cc and 500cc races, by less than a second in each event.

Les well and truly flying at something around 130mph, in practice for the 1952 Ulster Grand Prix. *FoTTofinders*

Landing heavily on the back tyre in practice, Les prepares for the large "tank-slapper" that usually followed the MV's leaps. Les advised Bill Lomas, riding an MV four for the first time at Ulster to hold lightly onto the bars to let the wobble correct itself. The extreme compression of front and rear suspension led to damage to the rear tyre in the race and Les had to abandon the race. *FoTTofinders*

Well ahead in the race, Les comes out of a corner perfectly lined up for maximum acceleration. One can only envy the four schoolboys. *FoTTofinders*

Les had a good race in the 250cc class, finishing third behind two Moto Guzzis. He replaced the "Oleo" telescopic forks and rear damper on the Velocette with girder front forks and Girling dampers at front and rear, and greatly improved the handling. *FoTTofinders*

Winning the Italian Grand Prix for MV made Les a popular hero among Italian motorcycle racing followers, and here Les and Edna enjoy the success that they had waited for so long after 1949.

Life in Italy – "Casa Gram"

Les' responsibilities as team manager, development engineer and racing motorcyclist for an Italian manufacturer left him little time to see his family in England, certainly not as much as he and Edna would have liked. Edna, and sometimes the boys, joined him for testing at Monza and Les stayed at home in Kent as much as he could between races. As it became clear during 1952 that MV offered him long term, stimulating and well-paid employment, he raised the subject of moving the family to Italy with Domenico Agusta. An extra attraction of working for MV was that Les was treated as part of the Agusta family, and his proposal was welcomed by all of them.

The family owned a large villa near to the village of Viggiu near Varese, close to Lake Lugano and the Swiss frontier. It was some distance by winding road from MV's centre of operations at Cascina Costa di Verghera, which in turn is near the town of Gallarate, and it had occasionally been used in Summer. Domenico offered the house to the Graham family, and when his offer was accepted, he had it redecorated and brought up to scratch. Edna was invited to visit the furniture and fabric shops of Lugano to order anything she thought suitable for the house. It is unlikely that she went on her own; probably Domenico's mother, the Contessa Giuseppina Agusta, went with her, for she became

The Spanish Grand Prix in October 1952 was the slowest race of the season, and here Les is winning it at 59.54 mph. The course twisted round Montjuich Park. The Italian grand Prix a few weeks earlier was the fastest of the season, with a winning average of 106.29.

very fond of Edna and her family.

The Contessa was the widow of Giovanni, the MV company's founder. She was still the energetic mother of her boys, all of whom lived within scolding distance. In fact Carrado, the youngest, was the only one who needed any scolding; his responsibilities at MV were the lightest of the four and Edna's sister classed him as a "tearaway." Domenico was a strong general manager, Vincenzo managed the sales department, and Mario was described as Group Coordinator. Vincenzo made Barbara think of Errol Flynn but she did not enlarge on this opinion. The important thing was that they all got on well with Les.

When the family moved in after the 1952 season, they found a housekeeper, Lena, and a gardener, Sergio, in residence. Signor Campani, a young university graduate, was taken on to continue the education of Stuart, 11, and Christopher, 7. It was thought that they would move on to the International School near Geneva later on. Every necessity was

provided, perhaps more than Edna would have wanted; at least she was able to go with Les to some of his races leaving her boys in good care. Having a housekeeper to clean and prepare meals was not something Edna was used to, and left her with time on her hands.

Meanwhile there was the excitement of Monza "autodrome", where MV shared the track with other Italian car and motorcycle manufacturers for testing. Les already knew several of the Grand Prix car drivers from earlier testing. He was friendly with Fangio and also Farina and Ascari, who admired and drove his new Jaguar Mark VII, then bought their own. The boys thought that Monza was lovely, less for the exciting machines that raced by on the track than for the green lizards that lived in the long grass. The boys did watch the cars and bikes as well and became familiar with men like Mike Hawthorn, Geoff Duke and the MV team riders. Stuart remembers that Fangio waved to them, probably from a Grand Prix Maserati, as he passed on the track. Christopher was old enough to cross-

Good friends. Les stands behind a hybrid MV four on test at Monza with Carlo Bandirola. Both came to MV at the beginning of 1952, speaking nothing of each other's language, but their eagerness to communicate produced great aptitude with sign language and quick learning. They spoke about everything including race-course collisions of the past. Cecil Sandford also found "Bandi" good company - "a super fella".

Enrico Lorenzetti looks thoughtful as he waits to start in an Italian Championship race in 1953. He nursed the four cylinder Guzzi to several wins in 1953 and 1954, and was a much respected, dry-humoured rider.

examine some of the drivers about their speed through Monza's fastest bend, and surprised them by being unimpressed.

Both boys rode on racing machines, sitting in front of Les and holding the handlebars. Chris had his first ride on an AJS when he was five and made a grab for the twistgrip and yanked it open. When Les regained control he was not pleased with Chris, one of very few times Chris saw him angry. Les let himself be taken right round Monza by Stuart on a 125cc racer, reaching a reported 90mph. By then Stuart was an experienced 11 year old rider, having started riding with Dad while Les was still working for AJS. It may seem surprising that Les took such apparent risks with his sons, but he knew what he was doing and they were great memories that they still have.

The boys also spent many hours at the factory, exploring the production lines and watching the craftsmen of the various departments at work. They were well known and made welcome while Les worked in the racing department on the latest developments planned for the works racing machines.

Les was deeply involved in an important development at MV toward the end of 1952. Lawrence "Larry" Bell, founder of the Bell Aircraft Corporation, was in Europe looking for manufacturers to build his helicopters, demand for which was booming. He approached Meccanica Verghesa as a possible partner, and Les, knowing Bell as the maker of the wartime Airocobra low-level fighter and the first American jet fighter, as well as having knowledge of aircraft from his own wartime experience, took an important part in the discussions. Discussions

became negotiations and ended with MV reviving aircraft manufacture at Cascina Costa to build Bell helicopters under licence.

Clearly a good team of managers looked after this operation, for soon after starting to make Bell helicopters, MV planned their own models. It was not long before MV were making good helicopters to their own design, as well as the Bell. Within very few years, the MV Agusta type A109 was much in demand, and the turnover from this branch of the company dwarfed the returns from motorcycles. The company moved on to become Europe's largest builder of helicopters, it started joint ventures with Westland Helicopters and GKN, and is now part of the impenetrable world of conglomerates. It would be exaggerating to say that all Les touched at MV turned to gold, but he certainly made a difference to the company.

Apart from the sheer success of his work, the nicest thing for Les in Italy was the warmth of the people, not only locally. The little boys were admired, offered sweets and pastries, and had their cheeks pinched ruthlessly by adoring Italian grannies. Barbara remembers a local restaurant/cafe whose proprietor asked Edna what the boys liked best. "Chocolate cake!" Next evening a large chocolate cake was on

Practice for the Italian national race at Faenza in Spring 1953. It looks early in the morning of a working day, with interested passers-by taking shelter behind trees. *Gianni Perrone*

display on the Grahams' table. Les and Edna tested it to make sure it was not too sickly and nearly reeled from the strength of alcohol in the rich confection. It was definitely too strong for children, but it was definitely not done to reject the cake, so Les and Edna bravely set to eating it. According to Barbara, it took several evenings to demolish it.

The Agusta family welcomed the Grahams to their homes, where their children played with the boys and the adults mixed English, Italian and sign language in conversation. Picnics were organised by the lake, where several kayaks were tied up for family use. Even Bandirola, once regarded by English riders as the menace of the tracks, was like an uncle to Christopher and Stuart.

The boys still have good recollections of Italy and the Italians they got to know and realise now what a privileged time it was. For Edna, there were moments when she would have preferred to have

been more involved in household matters But she enjoyed Les' success and the lifestyle, and they all enjoyed the visitors from Britain who could make the long journey. The scheme of things at MV and "Casa Gram" had much to recommend it.

Many of the visitors were from the motorcycle and national press, or were representatives of the suppliers who had known Les from at least the late 1940s. These technical representatives gave important help with sorting out problems at the race track, as they do now, and Les was as loyal to his friends from Dunlop, Lucas and BP as they were to him. It was this loyalty that kept Les on Dunlop tyres after Norton changed to Avons in 1950, and Dunlop made sure that the problems were solved. There was a financial element in this relationship, for many suppliers paid a bonus to riders who did well with their products. Les must have been one of the best paid British motorcycle racers of that time.

Race day at Faenza and Les MV has a new mudguard and mini-screen. His MV did not finish the race which was won by Colnago, Gilera. *Gianni Perrone*

The Final Year

MV's success in the last two Grand Prix races of 1952 galvanised Gilera into a thorough revision of their four cylinder racer for the new season. Alteration of the valve angles and camshafts as well as improved carburation brought the Gileras' power up to 60-plus at 10,500 rpm. The frame and brakes were also altered. Three Britons were engaged to ride for the company in 1953, Geoff Duke, Dickie Dale and Reg Armstrong. Duke was keen to ride for Norton, but only with a certainty, before long, of the competitive new four cylinder engine that never appeared. When Joe Craig told him that it was still an unborn baby, and Norton's chairman treated him like dirt, Duke accepted Gilera's offer of twice his Norton salary and no deduction of start money, as was the custom of some British firms.

Beside the three Britons, Pierre Monneret was promised a Gilera for major French events. As Gilera already employed Masetti, Milani, Colnago, Pagani

and occasionally Gianni and Liberati, as works riders, Masetti, World's Champion rider in 1952, was extremely annoyed. Taruffi was unable to appease the rider, so Masetti offered his services to MV.

MV seem to have made few changes to their "fours". Les now had himself, Bill Lomas, Bandirola and, on a short term basis, Masetti, to ride them. A very strong team of Ubialli, Cecil Sandford and Copeta were to handle the 125s, with Lomas when his NSU commitments allowed. Les was now seriously planning his retirement from motorcycle racing, to concentrate on team management and technical development for MV, and maybe to try car racing. While he had no interest in riding motorcycles on the road, he enjoyed using the speed of his Jaguar on the winding roads of the Varese area, and had impressed Aston Martin and Jaguar at his earlier driving trials.

He was 41, tough and fit, but aware that his energy

The 1953 Ultra-Lightweight TT. Les leaves Sulby Bridge on the 125cc single, which by now had eclipsed the Mondial and Morini 125s.

and will to win would not last for ever. Ken Kavanagh recalls meeting Les at a Southampton club dinner, and Les offering him a place in the MV team. Ken remembers answering "No, I'm a Norton man."

Moto Guzzi had worked hard on their machines. The 250 now had double overhead camshafts and a carburettor mounted almost vertically, feeding in a straight line through a huge inlet tract. A new, very complex-looking 500cc in-line four cylinder 500cc machine with a fuel system worthy of a Rolls Royce Merlin was tested at Monza early in the year and apparently went well. All the Guzzi machines had had wind-tunnel therapy, and carried light, simple but quite extensive streamlining.

MV did not do very well in the first races of the year. At Faenza, Colnago (Gilera) won, Les retired while in the lead and an angry Bandirola came third. He claimed that second-finisher Milani deliberately obstructed him and a protest was lodged and ignored. The new Guzzi won races at Mettet and Hockenheim, where Fergus Anderson lapped at 112.6 mph. Les did not finish. Ken Kavanagh and his Norton team-mate Sid Lawton won at Floreffe.

The Senior TT of 1953 had probably the largest

number of Italian machines ever entered up to this year. Four Gileras and two MVs were listed. Ken Kavanagh and Ray Amm on works Nortons were the fastest in practice at over 94 mph, while Duke and Armstrong on the Gileras, and Les on the MV, lapped around a steady 90 mph. MV had a 350cc four cylinder bike, with a scaled-down engine but the same frame and gearbox as the 500s. Les took this round in practice at 90mph as well, faster than any other 350 and close to the 350cc lap record. The machine that Les had prepared for himself to ride in the Senior race was much taller than his 1952 second place winner. Special long telescopic suspension units held the bike about 9 inches clear of the road; Les liked plenty of suspension travel, and in 1952 his exhaust pipes had grounded heavily enough to flatten them. The 1953 racer would not suffer from grounding, but must have needed quite a leap into the saddle when the engine fired.

The 350 MV suffered from clutch slip almost from the start of the Junior TT and completed only one lap. Rod Coleman led the race on the first lap, then Ray Amm caught up with him (on time - they could not see each other on the road.) Ken Kavanagh was a close second, and a safe distance from Amm, the rider he once described as "a dicer.... short circuit

Flat out on the back stretch between Ballacraine and Sulby, Les heads to the TT win that he had waited for patiently.

type of rider.... terribly, terribly dangerous to live with on big circuits." Rod Coleman did not agree; he said of Amm – "to say he was determined would be an understatement", and people were wrong to call him "wild" because he sometimes put his foot down. Ray Amm took a lead of 15 seconds from Kavanagh to win the race.

The "Ultra Lightweight" 125cc race was headed from start to finish by Les, to win a TT at long last. He was greeted by cheers from the crowd at the finish line. Werner Haas was second on an NSU, as he had been in the 250cc TT, two very good results on his first visit to the TT course.

Then came the Senior TT, with expectations of victory pretty evenly divided between Geoff Duke and Les, with Kavanagh and Ray Amm well in the running for a win. Ken Kavanagh was at the start near Les before they took up their positions for the interval start. He recalls:

"On the starting line for the Senior TT he asked if I had thought it over [joining MV]. I told Les like lots of us at Bracebridge Street, I was worried about the future at Norton after the sell out to Pearl Insurance. We had been put under the "protection" of A.M.C. I

was standing beside the MV and I said that I could never race a thing like this, the petrol filler was chest high on me... but Les said 'don't worry, for the TT I believe in long soft suspension... we'll talk about it later on.'... I never saw Les alive again."

The fastest riders had been given the following start numbers. Les, 18, Reg Armstrong, 28, Ken Kavanagh, 42, Ray Amm, 61, Geoff Duke, 67. Ken Kavanagh was worried that Duke would catch up with Amm on the road "and when Ray got Geoff in his sights he would go out of his mind." It seems there was good reason for his concern as Ray did everything possible to keep ahead of Duke when Geoff caught up, including drifting onto the grass on the side of some of the high-speed bends between Sulby and Ramsey. So Les was first of the fast men away from the start. Twenty four minutes later the MV roared past the grandstands and pits to start the second lap, and down Bray Hill. Then came appalling disaster.

As Les left the right hand kerb at the bottom of the hill and started up toward the Knoll and what is now called Ago's Leap, at around 130mph, the MV swerved violently to the left of the road, went over the curb and on to the footpath, where it crashed into the solid wall on the left, and Les and his machine

Coming away from Governor's Bridge on the way to Bray Hill. The elongated forks and suspension units show clearly in this side view. Les made this modification to give a flexible ride over the Isle of Man bumps without grounding the exhausts. In spite of its unwieldy appearance, Les impreoved on his time for the first lap of the 1952 TT by several seconds.

were carried by the huge momentum in a grinding slide for over 100 yards. Les did not have a chance, either to correct the sudden change of direction, nor to survive the violence of the crash.

For many shocked spectators that was the end of the race. For some it was the end of their interest in motorcycle racing, as many followers of the sport had concentrated their enthusiasm on the career of Les Graham. Needless to say many riders were horrified at the sight of the MV burning on the side of the road, and George Brown, who followed Les down Bray Hill, crashed into debris on the rise toward Quarter Bridge. He never returned to the Island.

Fortunately Les and Edna had not taken the boys to the TT. They were staying with Edna's parents, and when she was told of the accident she quickly got a message to her mother to make sure the boys did not pick up the news from the radio.

There is still uncertainty about what went wrong at the bottom of Bray Hill and there are still a surprising number of ex-riders and others who are sure that they know, but who cannot get proof that their particular theory is right. A mechanical failure seems almost certain, but it is for others more knowledgeable to say what actually failed. The race was won by Ray Amm, followed by Reg Armstrong on a Gilera.

The death of Les meant the end of the connection with MV and of living in Italy and the devastated family returned to England. Edna's sister Barbara and her husband Fred welcomed Edna and the boys to their home in Lincoln. Later they all moved to "the Rectory," in Stone in Staffordshire. It was a big house, large enough for each family to have their own accommodation, and Barbara and Fred had children quite close to Stuart and Christopher in age. A few years later Edna and the boys settled in Cheshire.

Fred undertook the dismal task of driving all the way to Gallarate and Viggiu in Les' Jaguar, with trailer. He made the journey with Edna to bring back the Grahams' belongings and to say goodbye to their friends at MV. They were met with the greatest sympathy and help from the Agusta family, who themselves were in mourning for Les. The racing

The final descent of Bray Hill before something threw the MV off-line just beyond the bottom of the Hill.

representatives of Dunlop, BP and other firms that had supplied parts and consumables to Les over the years were also most helpful with the transport of the Grahams' larger possessions back to England.

Of the boys, Stuart's memory is slightly blank for some of the months when he and Christopher were trying to absorb what had happened. Both were old enough to see and read bits in the press about the accident, with pointless and uninformed speculation about its causes. There were also photos from the accident scene which were painful to a casual reader, let alone a close relative of the victim and did nothing to help at a difficult time.

On the other hand tributes to the personality and achievements of Les poured into the motorcycle press and into the Grahams' home. About 400 friends and representatives of various clubs and organisations came to the funeral at Landican Cemetery near Birkenhead, many having to stand outside the chapel, which was full. There were all his former AJS team-mates, Corrado Agusta from MV, the head of the Italian motorcycle sport association, and a contingent from the Oswestry Club which included old rivals

from his first racing days; among 200 floral tributes were wreaths from the Federation Internationale Motorcycliste and one from the canteen staff at A.M.C.

Many riders put on record their appreciation of help they had received from Les in getting started, finding a good machine or with advice on dealing with tricky circuits or riding conditions. Others simply remembered what good company he was and were happy to have had such a friend. The Agusta family kept in contact for many years, with a bond that was strongest with Contessa Agusta until her death.

Under a photograph of Les with Ken Kavanagh and Cecil Sandford after the 1952 German Grand Prix, Ken has written: "Les always smiled like this; he was never long faced, he never criticised other riders, he was never angry. He was open and friendly with everybody, even Joe Craig and all the Norton team."

These comments expressed what almost every rider who met Les felt; he had an optimistic outlook that enabled him to shrug off bad luck, and he had an infectious enjoyment of life. He was not a great

The Last Post. Family members, racing colleagues and the representatives of several organisations stand at the formal opening of the Les Graham Memorial in 1955. It stands by The Verandah on the TT course, and besides recalling Les, it serves during TT races and practice as a shelter and communications centre.

practical joker, but he liked to lead on the innocent, as when he improved on a rumour that the new works AJS 350 had twin camshafts, telling the pressman who stopped him before a practice session – "Shhh! this one has three cams!"

During the war he took every opportunity of leave to visit Edna and his little boys. On evenings at base if there was not a bombing operation he enjoyed visiting the "Oswald" pub at Scunthorpe with his aircrew to urge on the amateur talent the pub encouraged. At the same time he was one of the Lancaster "Skippers" whose crew knew that they owed him their lives.

As a racing motorcyclist he was absolutely professional and a hard rider. For all his love of fun and acceptance of disappointments, he was a driven man. When he rode in a team he made sure that his bike was the best, or at least a very good one. He warned Bill Lomas that if he rode for a German or Italian team, he risked being fobbed off with the runt of the machinery unless he claimed a good machine and hung on to it.

Years of riding on a great variety of tracks, from speedway to quality tarmac, and in all kinds of weather, gave him a confidence in the wet and on gravel that was probably unique. He willingly passed on his tips for riding in bad conditions to young riders. On the race track he was ruthless if that was necessary to win. Like Rossi today, Les could find a way past a rival that nobody else saw, and on occasion he would use a little nudge to enlarge a narrow gap, but he was never the cause of an accident. In pre-war grass track physical contact was the norm and no one would say either rider was to blame.

His was a personality that would have made things happen in any walk of life. His iron determination, good humour, and an interest in seeing young contenders succeed were qualities that made him an icon of motorcycle sport.

Les' elder brother Versey was a sidecar winner at the May meeting at Donington in 1937. His passenger, unfortunately unknown, hangs on while Versey applies power to his Grindlay-JAP.

The Racing Grahams

The passing of Les did was not the end of motorcycle racing in the Graham family; it seems that speed is in the genes of the family. All three sons of Andrew and Emily loved racing, and three of the next generation were also successful in motorsport for at least part of their lives.

From their teens, around 1930, Versey, Les and Richard Graham were members of the Oswestry and District Motorcycle Club, and lived close enough to races at Park Hall, Chester and North Wales to make racing their regular weekend outing. Often all three went together with their girlfriends, who were their wives-to-be, and Richard's widow Della, known as

"Girlie" to the gang, remembers these outings.

The boys had a friend who was a butcher, and his father lent them his big van to transport them and Les and Versey's racing machines to the weekend events. Richard was as keen on racing as his brothers, but Emily Graham, a woman of intelligence and strong opinions, decided that two out of three sons risking their neck by racing motorcyles was enough, and Richard was barred from racing. Richard, or his brothers for him, decided that this ban did not include going as passenger for Versey in sidecar races, and he performed well on a sidecar that provided little more than a platform to perch on and a pole sticking up

Versey's son Jim with the 50cc special that he created at the age of sixteen. It used a Cucciolo engine, the Rolls-Royce of cyclemotor power-units, made by Ducati.

through the middle of it to cling on to while hanging out at corners. Les and Versey's wife also took a turn in the sidecar on occasions, (though not at the same time).

Of course the time came when "Rich", as he was called, fell out of the sidecar heavily enough to necessitate a visit to Oswestry hospital in the butcher's van. He had broken his collar bone on a track corner post. Apparently a story was invented to explain the injury when the brothers got home.

As Versey and Les got more experienced and successful, they did not always travel to the same meetings. Versey started racing on solos but concentrated on sidecars when he realised that he had a gift for them. He had most of his success on a sidecar outfit powered by a 596cc JAP engine and built by a Mr Grindley who at a workshop at Preese Heath in Shropshire. Grindley built more than one outfit and lent some of them out. Former grass-tracker Eric Atherton remembers "old man" Grindley at races tearing a strip off sidecarrists who used his outfits but fell short of his expectations.

Versey faced stiff opposition in sidecar racing. On road courses, including Donington and Cadwell, Arthur Horton, Henry Laird (Morgan) and Len Taylor were among the hottest on three wheels. Others like Jack Surtees, Tommy Deadman and Eric Oliver raced solos or sidecars wherever they thought it was worth while, be it grass or road. Versey also raced on both but won more often on the road. When Les went to ride in the TT in 1938 and 1939, Versey went with him as helper and pit attendant. He went to all the postwar TT races up to 1953; he was shattered by Les' death, lost interest in racing and never went to the Isle of Man again.

His son Jim was the first of the next generation to take up motorcycle racing. He started on grass track when living in Amesbury, after a series of family moves from Wallasey, where he was born. With the start of 50cc racing in Britain, Jim built himself a neat racer, fitting a Cucciolo OHV cyclemotor engine into a much-modified cycle frame, for which he made the front and rear suspension and a six-speed gear system. The "Cucciolo" engine was the first post-war product of the Ducati factory, and possibly the only engine ever to have pullrods rather than pushrods. It

The fast Ariel Arrow assembled and tuned by Hermann Meier which Jim Graham raced in 1959 and 1960.

provided good motive power for Jim's "special."

Jim moved up to Aermacchis provided by Bill Webster, a good friend of Les and the Graham family, but soon a job at Lawton and Wilson's large motorcycle agency, where he rose to Sales Manager, provided him with a choice of racing machines from stock or work in progress. He also rode an Ariel Arrow two-stroke racer built by Hermann Meier in 1959 and 1960 – a machine that pioneered some of the intake/exhaust resonance principles that made later two-strokes go so fast.

Jim was a regular competitor in the Isle of Man South West 100 near Castletown. Starting in 1963 he continued to race there regularly until 1993, when, as Jim put it, "they found out how old I was!" By then he knew the circuit pretty well and had set several lap records.

He decided to enter the Manx Grand Prix for the first time in the same year, having missed the TT for personal and business reasons, and won Best Newcomer award. Jim's motorcycle racing career was even longer than that of Les, and his enthusiasm for the sport is undiminished.

Stuart Graham's first contact with anything related to motorcycle racing was on his third birthday, when his parents gave him a tricycle which Les had arranged to be painted in the handsome shade of blue unique to the OK Supreme road racers of the 30s.

When Les died Stuart was 11 and Christopher was 8. As they grew up their enthusiasm for cars and motorcycles increased and developed into a desire to race. When Stuart entered his first event at Oulton Park when he was 19, Edna asked Crewe-based dealer and former racer Bill Webster to keep an eye on the boys' enthusiasm. When Stuart showed promise Bill decided to support him on the Aermacchis that he was importing.

Stuart recalls: "Mother was not keen, understandably, but felt I might be safer on the track than on the road. She no doubt felt my enthusiasm was inevitable but hoped it would wear off, but she was very understanding, and later, when I was successful, I think she was proud and knew Dad would have been too. But she was immensely relieved when I retired from bike racing."

By 1966 Stuart had made his mark on the motorcycle racing world and was successful enough to leave Rolls Royce, where both he and Christopher had enjoyed their formal training and experience. He set out to make a living as a full-time professional in Grand Prix racing, taking with him his young wife

Jim on one of many Aermacchis that he rode successfully from the 1960s to the 1990s. He is at the hairpin on the Castletown road course on the Isle of Man during one of the Southern 100 meetings.

Margaret, a van and caravan and a well-prepared Matchless G50 and an AJS 7R.

He did startlingly well in most of his races, including second place to Agostini in the Belgian Grand Prix in heavy rain. Only midway through his first Grand Prix season, with a recommendation from Mike Hailwood, Stuart joined the Honda team to ride the 250cc six-cylinder racer, a much faster and more difficult machine than the Matchless - and a real challenge on the fast, dangerous circuits of the 1960s. Having mastered the machines and the circuits Stuart achieved excellent results, including second place to Hailwood in the 1966 250cc TT. His performance and ability to come to terms with difficult machines showed he had the toughness and natural flair of his father.

In 1967 Stuart joined the Suzuki works team, and having adapted to the astronomical revs and tiny powerbands of the Japanese two-strokes, had a successful year, which included winning his first TT on a 50cc Suzuki at over 85mph and taking second place in the 125cc race. To win a TT, as

Les had done fourteen years earlier, had a very special significance to the Graham family.

When the Japanese factories pulled out of racing in 1968, Stuart still had a contract with Suzuki, and raced on in selected events on a Suzuki-suplied racer. By now Stuart was thinking of his future and bought a small garage near Nantwich. After practicing for the 1970 TT in foul conditions on a 500cc Suzuki, he decided to retire from motorcycle racing and concentrate on the business.

While establishing the garage business with brother Chris, Stuart entered saloon car racing, and became the man to beat in Chevrolet Camaros with engines built by Chris, and in works Ford Capris. He won several saloon racing championships and became the only man after Freddie Dixon to win both the motorcycle and car TT races. Stuart still drives in some of the major Historic motorsport events, and to see him sliding a big Lister-Chevrolet or Ferrari into one of the corners at Goodwood shows that his competitive urge is as strong as ever.

Stuart Graham rides the 1952 MV racer between races at Boreham. He is ten, and going fast enough for the background to be blurred. Les looks fairly calm.

Christopher, his quiet and intensely enthusiastic brother, also has the Graham flair for speed. At his mother's request, supported by that of his wife Rosemary, Chris has refrained from motorcycle racing. His aunt Barbara who has known him from birth describes him as totally fearless and fast on whatever wheels he could find when a boy. Stuart agrees that Chris could have been a world-beater too on motorcycles, though perhaps total fearlessness is not always an advantage.

As a safer alternative to motorcycle racing Chris took up Kart racing, and was only deprived of the 1973 British Kart championship on his Suzuki-powered machine by a blown tyre. Chris built and tuned the 250cc engine of his kart, one of the fastest in the UK.

Chris became an engine builder at Rolls Royce, assembling the V8 engines fitted to their saloon cars. This skill was a major asset in building the mighty engines for Stuart's Camaro, and later Lola GT. Other Camaro engine users, from endurance

racers to off-shore powerboat racers have come to Chris to have engines rebuilt and prepared for their particular branch of motorsport. Chris releases his urge for speed on two wheels with occasional track days, mostly with a Honda Fireblade. He also has a jewel – like MV Agusta strictly for dry road runs. This machine was built specially for Chris by MV after he visited the factory and was welcomed by the present management. Chris is an artist as well as an engineer, and this motorcycle perfectly combines art and engineering.

After Chris joined Graham in the Garage enterprise, with hard work and the help of their wives, they developed the business into a major Honda car agency with a second branch at Aston near Nantwich. The business was sold in 2001 but continues under the Stuart Graham name. Stuart and Chris live near to each other in countryside near Nantwich. They have seen and taken part in racing very different from that of today, but they are still very much part of today's motorsport world.

Just fourteen years later Stuart is in the top ranks of international riders. He was second in the 1966 250cc TT with this 6-cylinder factory Honda to Mike Hailwood, who introduced him to Honda.

Stuart won the 50cc TT and came second to Phil Read in the 125cc race in 1967, riding factory Suzuki two-strokes with lots of power in a very narrow band. This is the 125cc model with which he averaged an almost identical speed to the 6-cylinder Honda in 1966.

Chris Graham raced in the top division of Kart racing, using Karts powered by Suzuki engines he had assembled. He missed the 1973 National Kart Championship by a piece of bad luck.

The Bimota which Chris used to run on track days. He now runs a Honda Fireblade for these events.

A cheery group waiting to start practice for the 1949 Ulster Grand Prix; No. 5 Harold Daniell, Senior Norton, No. 3 Bob Foster, Senior Moto Guzzi, No. 42 Ted Frend, Junior AJS. *FoTTofinders*

Race Results

Les Graham – International Grands Prix and TTs

1936
250cc Ulster Grand Prix. .... Did not finish

1937
250cc Ulster Grand Prix. .... 4th OK Supreme

1938
250cc Isle of Man TT .... 13th OK Supreme

1939
250cc Isle of Man TT .... Did not finish

1947
500cc Isle of Man TT .... 9th AJS
500cc Ulster Grand Prix .... Did not finish

Harold Daniell, looking very fresh, perhaps after a bath, on a "featherbed" Norton before the 1950 TT. *FoTTofinders*

1948

350cc Swiss Grand Prix	6th AJS
500cc Swiss Grand Prix	Did not finish
350cc Isle of Man TT	7th AJS
500cc Isle of Man TT	Did not finish
350cc Belgian GP	Did not finish
500cc Belgian GP	Did not finish
500cc Ulster Grand Prix	3rd AJS

1949

350cc Swiss Grand Prix	2nd AJS
500cc Swiss Grand Prix	1st AJS
350cc Isle of Man TT	Did not finish
500cc Isle of Man TT	10th AJS
350cc Dutch TT	Did not finish
500cc Dutch TT	2nd AJS
350cc Belgian Grand Prix	Did not finish
500cc Belgian Grand Prix	Did not finish
500cc Ulster Grand Prix	1st AJS
500cc Italian Grand Prix	Did not finish

Ray Amm on Bray Hill 1953 – always brave, always fast – some thought he was sometimes dangerous.

1950

350cc Isle of Man TT	4th AJS
500cc Isle of Man TT	4th AJS
350cc Belgian Grand Prix	Did not finish
500cc Belgian Grand Prix	Did not finish
350cc Dutch TT	Did not finish
500cc Dutch TT	Did not finish
350cc Swiss Grand Prix	1st AJS
500cc Swiss Grand Prix	1st AJS
500cc Ulster Grand Prix	2nd AJS
350cc Italian Grand Prix	2nd AJS
500cc Italian Grand Prix	7th AJS

1951

350cc Swiss Grand Prix	1st Velocette
500cc Swiss Grand Prix	Did not finish
125cc Isle of Man TT	Did not finish (MV)
350cc Isle of Man TT	10th Velocette
500cc Isle of Man TT	Did not finish (MV)
350cc Belgian Grand Prix	10th Velocette
500cc Belgian Grand Prix	Did not finish
125cc Dutch TT	3rd MV Agusta
350cc Dutch TT	Did not finish
500cc Dutch TT	Did not finish
350cc Italian Grand Prix	7th Velocette
500cc Italian Grand Prix	Did not start

Did not start in any class of Spanish or French Grands Prix.

The kind of bump that produced high-speed tank-slappers on the Clady Straight. Les in practice on an Earles Fork model. *FoTTofinders*

1952

250cc Swiss Grand Prix	3rd Benelli
500cc Swiss Grand Prix	Did not finish
250cc Isle of Man TT	4th Velocette
350cc Isle of Man TT	Did not finish
500cc Isle of Man TT	2nd MV Agusta
125cc Dutch TT	Did not finish
350cc Dutch TT	7th Velocette
500cc Dutch TT	7th MV Agusta
350cc Belgian Grand Prix	6th Velocette
500cc Belgian Grand Prix	Did not finish
350cc German Grand Prix	Did not finish
500cc German Grand Prix	4th MV Agusta
250cc Ulster Grand Prix	3rd Velocette
500cc Ulster Grand Prix	Did not finish
125cc Italian Grand Prix	3rd MV Agusta
500cc Italian Grand Prix	1st MV Agusta
125cc Spanish Grand Prix	3rd MV Agusta
500cc Spanish Grand Prix	1st MV Agusta

1953

125cc Isle of Man TT	1st MV Agusta
500cc Isle of Man TT	Did not finish

Index